The Commedia dell'Arte

Forms of Drama

Forms of Drama meets the need for accessible, mid-length volumes that offer undergraduate readers authoritative guides to the distinct forms of global drama. From classical Greek tragedy to Chinese pear garden theatre, cabaret to *kathakali*, the series equips readers with models and methodologies for analysing a wide range of performance practices and engaging with these as 'craft'.

SERIES EDITOR: SIMON SHEPHERD

Cabaret
978-1-3501-4025-7
William Grange

Classical Greek Tragedy
978-1-3501-4456-9
Judith Fletcher

Pageant
978-1-3501-4451-4
Joan FitzPatrick Dean

Romantic Comedy
978-1-3501-8337-7
Trevor R. Griffiths

Satire
978-1-3501-4007-3
Joel Schechter

Tragicomedy
978-1-3501-4430-9
Brean Hammond

The Commedia dell'Arte

Domenico Pietropaolo

methuen | drama

LONDON • NEW YORK • OXFORD • NEW DELHI • SYDNEY

METHUEN DRAMA
Bloomsbury Publishing Plc
50 Bedford Square, London, WC1B 3DP, UK
1385 Broadway, New York, NY 10018, USA
29 Earlsfort Terrace, Dublin 2, Ireland

BLOOMSBURY, METHUEN DRAMA and the Methuen Drama logo are
trademarks of Bloomsbury Publishing Plc

First published in Great Britain 2022

ISBN: HB: 978-1-3501-4419-4
        PB: 978-1-3501-4418-7
        ePDF: 978-1-3501-4421-7
        ePUB: 978-1-3501-4420-0

Series: Forms of Drama

Typeset by Integra Software Services Pvt. Ltd.

For Laura

CONTENTS

FIGURES

SERIES PREFACE

The scope of this series is scripted aesthetic activity that works by means of personation.

Scripting is done in a wide variety of ways. It may, most obviously, be the more or less detailed written text familiar in the stage play of the western tradition, which not only provides lines to be spoken but directions for speaking them. Or it may be a set of instructions, a structure or scenario, on the basis of which performers improvise, drawing, as they do so, on an already learnt repertoire of routines and responses. Or there may be nothing written, just sets of rules, arrangements and even speeches orally handed down over time. The effectiveness of such unwritten scripting can be seen in the behaviour of audiences, who, without reading a script, have learnt how to conduct themselves appropriately at the different activities they attend. For one of the key things that unwritten script specifies and assumes is the relationship between the various groups of participants, including the separation, or not, between doers and watchers.

What is scripted is specifically an aesthetic activity. That specification distinguishes drama from non-aesthetic activity using personation. Following the work of Erving Goffman in the mid-1950s, especially his book *The Presentation of Self in Everyday Life*, the social sciences have made us richly aware of the various ways in which human interactions are performed. Going shopping, for example, is a performance in that we present a version of ourselves in each encounter we make. We may indeed have changed our clothes before setting out. This, though, is a social performance.

The distinction between social performance and aesthetic activity is not clear-cut. The two sorts of practice overlap and mingle with one another. An activity may be more or less aesthetic, but the crucial distinguishing feature is the status of the aesthetic element. Going shopping may contain an aesthetic element – decisions about clothes and shoes to wear – but its purpose is not deliberately to make an aesthetic activity or to mark itself as different from everyday social life. The aesthetic element is not regarded as a general requirement. By contrast a court-room trial may be seen as a social performance, in that it has an important social function, but it is at the same time extensively scripted, with prepared speeches, costumes and choreography. This scripted aesthetic element assists the social function in that it conveys a sense of more than everyday importance and authority to proceedings which can have life-changing impact. Unlike the activity of going shopping the aesthetic element here is not optional. Derived from tradition it is a required component that gives the specific identity to the activity.

It is defined as an activity in that, in a way different from a painting of Rembrandt's mother or a statue of Ramesses II, something is made to happen over time. And, unlike a symphony concert or firework display, that activity works by means of personation. Such personation may be done by imitating and interpreting – 'inhabiting' – other human beings, fictional or historical, and it may use the bodies of human performers or puppets. But it may also be done by a performer who produces a version of their own self, such as a stand-up comedian or court official on duty, or by a performer who, through doing the event, acquires a self with special status as with the *hijras* securing their sacredness by doing the ritual practice of *badhai*.

Some people prefer to call many of these sorts of scripted aesthetic events not drama but cultural performance. But there are problems with this. First, such labelling tends to keep in place an old-fashioned idea of western scholarship that drama, with its origins in ancient Greece, is a specifically European 'high' art. Everything outside it is then potentially, and damagingly, consigned to a domain which may be neither 'art' nor 'high'. Instead the European stage play and its like can best be regarded as a subset of the general category, distinct from the rest in that two groups of people come together in order specifically to present and watch a story being acted out by imitating other persons and settings. Thus the performance of a stage play in this tradition consists of two levels of activity using personation: the interaction of audience and performers and the interaction between characters in a fictional story.

The second problem with the category of cultural performance is that it downplays the significance and persistence of script, in all its varieties. With its roots in the traditional behaviours and beliefs of a society script gives specific instructions for the form – the materials, the structure and sequence – of the aesthetic activity, the drama. So too, as we have noted, script defines the relationships between those who are present in different capacities at the event.

It is only by attending to what is scripted, to the form of the drama, that we can best analyse its functions and pleasures. At its most simple, analysis of form enables us to distinguish between different sorts of aesthetic activity. The masks used in *kathakali* look different from those used in commedia dell'arte. They are made of different materials, designs and colours. The roots of those differences lie in their separate cultural traditions and systems of living. For similar reasons the puppets of *karagoz* and *wayang* differ. But perhaps more importantly the attention to form provides a basis for exploring the operation and effects of a particular work. Those who regularly participate in and watch drama, of whatever sort, learn to recognize and remember the forms of what they see and hear. When one drama has family resemblances to another, in its organization and use of materials, structure and sequences, those who attend it develop expectations as to how it will – or indeed should – operate. It then becomes possible to specify how a particular work subverts, challenges or enhances these expectations.

Expectation doesn't only govern response to individual works, however. It can shape, indeed has shaped, assumptions about which dramas are worth studying. It is well established that Asia has ancient and rich dramatic traditions, from the Indian sub-continent to Japan, as does Europe, and these are studied with enthusiasm. But there is much less widespread activity, at least in western universities, in relation to the traditions of, say, Africa, Latin America and the Middle East. Secondly, even within the recognized traditions, there are assumptions that some dramas are more 'artistic', or indeed more 'serious', 'higher' even, than others. Thus it may be assumed that *noh* or classical tragedy will require the sort of close attention to craft which is not necessary for mumming or *badhai*.

Both sets of assumptions here keep in place a system which allocates value. This series aims to counteract a discriminatory value system by ranging as widely as possible across world practices and by giving the same sort of attention to all the forms it features. Thus book-length studies of forms such as *al-halqa*, *hana keaka* and *ta'zieh* will appear in English for perhaps the first time. Those studies, just like those of *kathakali*, tragicomedy and the rest, will adopt the same basic approach. That approach consists of an historical overview of the development of a form combined with, indeed anchored in, detailed analysis of examples and case studies. One of the benefits of properly detailed analysis is that it can reveal the construction which gives a work the appearance of being serious, artistic, and indeed 'high'.

What does that work of construction is script. This series is grounded in the idea that all forms of drama have script of some kind and that an understanding of drama, of any sort, has to include analysis of that script. In taking this approach, books in this series again challenge an assumption that has in recent times governed the study of drama. Deriving from the supposed, but artificial, distinction between cultural performance and drama, many accounts of cultural performance ignore its scriptedness and assume that the proper way of studying it is simply to describe how its practitioners behave and what they make. This is useful enough, but to leave it at that is to produce something that looks like a form of lesser anthropology. The description of behaviours is only the first step in that it establishes what the script is. The next step is to analyse how the script and form work and how they create effect.

But it goes further than this. The close-up analyses of materials, structures and sequences – of scripted forms – show how they emerge from and connect deeply back into the modes of life and belief to which they are necessary. They tell us in short why, in any culture, the drama needs to be done. Thus by adopting the extended model of drama, and by approaching all dramas in the same way, the books in this series aim to tell us why, in all societies, the activities of scripted aesthetic personation – dramas – keep happening, and need to keep happening.

I am grateful, as always, to Mick Wallis for helping me to think through these issues. Any clumsiness or stupidity is entirely my own.

Simon Shepherd

ACKNOWLEDGEMENTS

In the past couple of years, I have had occasion to discuss some of the issues in this book with various colleagues, including Erith Jaffe-Berg, Rosalind Kerr, Kyna Hamill and Gabrielle Houle. I am grateful to them for their thoughtful comments, which have helped me express my ideas more clearly.

At Bloomsbury I owe a debt of gratitude to Mark Dudgeon, publisher for Theatre and Shakespeare Studies, for his strong support of the project. I am also grateful to Ella Wilson and Lara Bateman for their thoughtful assistance at various stages, and to Joanne Rippin, Dawn Cunneen and the members of the production team for all their expert suggestions. I would also like to express my gratitude to Bloomsbury's anonymous readers for their comments and recommendations.

Gratitude of an entirely different order is due to Simon Shepherd, who first shared with me his editorial plan for a series of volumes on drama focused on dramaturgy and aesthetics. I am deeply grateful to him for including a volume on commedia dell'arte in his plan and for encouraging me to write it.

In this and other projects, my most supportive and most critical reader has been my wife, Laura Pietropaolo. I am grateful to her for her patience, her understanding of the issues examined in the book, her always sharp criticism and her many constructive suggestions along the way.

Introduction

The expression commedia dell'arte refers to an Italian actor-centred theatre practice from the second half of the sixteenth century to the last decades of the eighteenth, followed by a succession of revivals and adaptations in later periods of history down to the present. The commedia dell'arte made its first appearance in Italy but soon entered the theatre markets of other European countries, most notably France, and eventually crossed the Atlantic to the New World. This historical purview of commedia dell'arte is uncontroversial in its generality, but precisely what kind of theatre practice was designated by the label is not as easily settled. Within that wide purview, many narrower views are possible, depending on the period of history, geographical area and primary sources we may be willing to privilege.

In a common interpretation, commedia dell'arte represents the performances of incorporated professionals in the commercial theatre or in court settings, as distinct from the activities of amateurs producing drama for diversion and education in various institutional contexts, and mountebanks performing in streets and marketplaces. In this view, the professional actors of the commedia dell'arte had no restrictions of dramatic form, being able to perform in virtually all genres with and without scripts, from the broad comedy of masked characters to lyrical pastoral and tragedy. A primary source of privilege in this approach is *La supplica* (*The Supplication*, 1634), a defence of the acting profession authored by the distinguished actor Niccolò Barbieri, for whom the term 'commedia' itself covers all the dramatic genres, serious as well as comic. It is clear that in such a view, authoritatively championed in our times by Siro Ferrone, improvisation, which for many is virtually synonymous with the best of commedia dell'arte, is a common but not a necessary feature of its practice.

For scholars at the other end of the spectrum, commedia dell'arte designates no more than a comic genre performed on the basis of an unscripted scenario. The most famous primary source behind this view is *Il teatro comico* (*The Comic Theatre*, 1750), a metatheatrical play by Carlo Goldoni, for whom plays in the commedia dell'arte tradition were based on the skill of improvisatory players. It is equally clear that, in this view, the defining features of commedia dell'arte include rigid genre restrictions and composition of the performance text by direct improvisation. From the early twentieth century to the present, this end of the spectrum has been the starting point of a remarkably heterogeneous group of commedia scholars, including rigorous students of improvisation as a disciplined, memory-based and highly regulated composition of the performance text, as well as the odd misguided romantic for whom improvisation means spontaneous creativity *ex nihilo*.

Between the two polarities of the scholarly spectrum, it is possible to identify various other perspectives – each grounded in a different selection of primary sources – along a gradient of increasing generic inclusivity, varying reliance on strictly improvisational practices, and openness to the influence of street performances. In the theatre culture of the seventeenth and much of the eighteenth centuries, talented professionals and amateurs did not always operate in isolation from marketplace performers, who practised their art, in a survival economy, as small companies on the social margins of official theatres. Famous actors, as Robert Henke has compellingly argued, straddled 'plebeian and elite culture' (Henke 2016: 180). Between the methods of marketplace troupes and those of professional and amateur companies there was considerable if uneasy interaction well into the eighteenth century. In his self-tutoring as a playwright, Goldoni, as we shall see, made a concerted effort to study the performance and dramaturgical techniques of street theatre, confident that this would help him create characters and develop effective stage actions. The contact between marketplace and legitimate theatre has led M. A. Katritzky (2006: 40) to propose an alternative and eminently rational approach to the study of the commedia dell'arte tradition. It is based on the recognition that mountebanks contributed in a substantial way to the development of commedia dell'arte performance conventions and forms practised by professionals.

Common to all of these approaches is the idea that practitioners were players who, either literally or ideally, belonged to the profession, for professional guild or corporation is the source meaning of the Italian *arte* throughout the golden age of commedia dell'arte. Professionalism, however, presupposes the prior acquisition of skill through apprenticeship and training as well as possession of the technical knowledge required to yield a product of high quality. On this consideration, *arte* has also a secondary aesthetic meaning, a meaning analogous to the notion described in Aristotle's *Rhetoric* (54a10) as *techne,* a term that designates the technical knowledge of the art needed by an orator to make a fine speech and, by extension, by an actor to give an excellent performance. *Arte* signifies both the technical knowledge of the process and the aesthetic quality of the product.

The combination of primary and secondary senses of the term confers on the commedia dell'arte a semantic ambivalence that allows different orientations of scholarship. In his aesthetics of artistic form, the philosopher Luigi Pareyson argues that, while a practitioner can employ exact technical knowledge of an art to produce an object (*fare con arte*), another can use the same knowledge with aesthetic creativity, producing a work of art (*fare dell'arte*). These activities are the ends of a spectrum in which artisanship progressively approaches art (Pareyson 2009: 235).

In the commedia dell'arte, the ambivalence of *arte* covers the spectrum from craft to art, or from technical to aesthetic skill. In the theatre, technical skill that is purposely directed to the achievement of an aesthetic goal is the stuff of dramaturgy, understood as the conscious ordering of text and stage activities to generate an intellectually rewarding audience reception. Commedia dell'arte performances aimed to offer the audience agreeable entertainment while seeking to influence their view of society, chiefly, but not exclusively, by means of the ludicrous.

The present book examines the practice of commedia dell'arte in its historical evolution, paying special attention to its main dramatic forms, the material conditions of its performances and its place in the living culture of its time. In a commedia dell'arte play, the characters can be identified visually, verbally and functionally by the costumes they wear, the vernacular they speak and the dramatic role they have in the development of the action. Commedia performances make dramaturgical use of visual, verbal and actantial codes of signification and communication, the foundations of which will be explored in the chapters that follow.

In order to outline the identities of the characters with reliable accuracy, a clear distinction will be drawn between the type of commedia dell'arte that was prevalent in Northern Italy and the type that dominated the stage in Southern Italy. From their place of origin, these varieties of commedia dell'arte migrated throughout the regions of the peninsula and beyond to other countries, where prolonged contact with theatre cultures distinct from the one in which they were rooted changed them into other dramatic forms. Largely in virtue of this contact, commedia dell'arte began to explore other dramaturgies and other varieties of aesthetic experience.

PART ONE

Form, dramaturgy and content of early commedia dell'arte

1

The first professionals

Prehistory

The literary antecedents of the commedia dell'arte can be traced all the way back to Roman comedy through the genre of *commedia erudita* or learned comedy, which flourished in the sixteenth century, chiefly in academic and courtly circles. Adopting the dramatic form of Terence's plays, *commedia erudita* consisted of fully scripted comedies using material derived from literary works in Latin or Italian, structured in accordance with classical dramatic theory. Commedia dell'arte has much in common with *commedia erudita*, but it is with plays from another scripted genre, the vernacular comedy of the same period, that commedia dell'arte has the greatest affinity and to which its development is connected by clear lines of continuity, in the Northern states of the Italian peninsula, most notably in the Republic of Venice, as well as in the Kingdom of Naples in the South. In Northern Italy, the vernacular comedies of Angelo Beolco, known as Ruzante, and Andrea Calmo, both actors and playwrights, figure prominently in the prehistory of commedia dell'arte. The features of Ruzante's style of greatest interest consist of his use of the dialect of Padua rather than literary Tuscan, his notorious use of expletives and the coarse humour that he aimed to generate. His treatment of rustic love in a carnivalesque setting and his use of a low-register variety of dialect are typical of his entire production and are closely related to the early repertoire of the commedia dell'arte. In *L'Anconitana,* for example, the role of the protagonist is virtually that of a commedia dell'arte rustic servant (Fido 1973: 212), known later as a *zanni.* The French director Jacques Copeau saw the similarities between commedia dell'arte and this play, and in 1927 decided to stage it in a way that made the lineage clear (Rudlin 1986: 95). In addition to the preference for a local vernacular and a crudely realistic style, Beolco's chief legacy to the commedia dell'arte was a dramatic model for the role of the early *zanni.*

A similar influence on early commedia dell'arte was exercised by Andrea Calmo. Himself under the influence of Ruzante, Calmo was chronologically closer to the commedia dell'arte. A number of his characters may be regarded as antecendents of main figures of the commedia dell'arte, including Pantalone, Brighella and the Capitano. One of the most significant features that his plays had in common with the commedia dell'arte was the multilingual setting of the dramatic action, which included even some Greek, inspired, no doubt, by the Greek-speaking neighbourhoods of Venice. Calmo approached the theatre simultaneously as a playwright, as an actor and as a business man acutely aware of the commercial possibilities of the stage. He wrote plays that could be performed with a minimum of rehearsal time, composed of scenes that allowed for considerable enrichment by virtuosic improvisation directly on stage. This approach to theatre was decidedly anticlassical, in the sense that it encouraged the development of an actor-centred rather than a text-centred conception of performance (Castagno 1994: 50–1). Calmo shifted the focus from the literary playwright to the actor, emphasizing the creative role of the latter within the framework provided by the former. This was without doubt his greatest legacy to the Venetian commedia dell'arte.

In Southern Italy, the vernacular comedy that dominates the immediate prehistory of the commedia dell'arte includes the popular genre known as *farsa cavaiola.* The adjective *cavaiola* in the designation of the genre refers to the city of Cava, whose inhabitants were derided by the citizens of nearby Salerno as foolish, uncouth and clumsy simpletons, who spoke an equally unpolished dialect. The rivalry between Cava and Salerno may have been the origin of the *farse cavaiole*, but the derision of the inhabitants of Cava soon became just a literary convention of the genre and eventually lost its municipal specificity. The genre flourished in the fifteenth and sixteenth centuries, but by the end of the sixteenth century the circle of its dramatis personae was opened up to include masked characters from local carnival celebrations.

The *cavaiola* legacy included the notion of awkward and foolish characters, brawls and beatings, multilingual dialogue and derisive geographical stereotypes. We can find all of these elements in *La scola cavajola* by Giovanni D'Antonio, also known as Il Partenopeo, from Partenope, an ancient and now literary name for the city of Naples. *La scola cavajola* is a dramatic caricature of a rowdy school in Naples. The play is multilingual, and, despite the title, the characters no longer have any recognizable reference to Cava: the Teacher (Mastro) speaks Neapolitan and pig Latin, Pulcinella (Polecenella in the text) speaks Neapolitan, as do Zeza and Coviello, though the latter mixes dialect and Latin, while Giangurgolo performs his part in Calabrian and the Dottore speaks Bergamask hybridized with Latin. The unruly coexistence of a plurality of languages in the same community and the constant prospect of a fall into Babelian confusion are intended to bewilder the audience with humour and determine the quality of their aesthetic experience of the play. The diverse origin of the characters and their multilingual environment reflect the demographic reality of Naples, in which inhabitants from many small towns along the Tyrrhenian coast of Southern Italy, from the tip of Calabria to Salerno and beyond, had immigrated to Naples to escape incursions by pirates from north Africa and the eastern Mediterranean. The plot includes comic routines typical of later commedia dell'arte, such as a horseplay scene in which Pulcinella mounts Giangurgolo and rides him like a steed (D'Antonio 1788: 197). The foolishness and plebeian manners once used to satirize only the inhabitants of Cava were transplanted into a different social reality, grafted onto characters of a different origin, and were destined to become an integral part of the commedia dell'arte of Naples.

The first companies

One of the most distinctive features of the commedia dell'arte is its commercial base, the fact that the actors were organized into companies for the first time. In general, a commedia dell'arte performance was not the work of a group of actors brought together for that specific purpose, but the work of an organized company, actors who had incorporated themselves into troupes, held together by their commitment to a shared purpose and their agreement to contribute their individual talents to the collective creativity and commercial success of the company. The commedia dell'arte is a professional endeavour of companies, an area of the entertainment industry in which the principal constitutive unit is the company rather than the individual (Ferrone 2014: 25). In the commedia dell'arte the rise to stardom and the achievement of prosperity was a collective endeavour. The advantages of a professional company structure were numerous. Companies guaranteed a calendar of performances, added a sense of stability to individual careers, facilitated the attainment of high-level sponsorships and offered income security in case of illness. There were, of course, highly paid and much admired players working outside the commedia dell'arte network, but within its domain, the success of a show was the success of a company working as a corporate unit under the leadership of its director, who was both its business manager and the artistic supervisor or dramaturgical co-ordinator of its performances.

These ideas are all outlined in the earliest known legal document in the history of professional companies: a contract dated 25 February 1545 and signed in the presence of a notary public by eight actors who thereby incorporated themselves into a company, described as a 'fraternal compagnia' or a professional brotherhood (text in Oreglia 1968: 140–3). Under the leadership of one of the actors, Maphio Zanini, they all pledged to work together in harmony as a company of brothers, with a calendar of events for one entire year, minus the Lenten period and Easter octave. The expression 'fraternal compagnia' was no more than a descriptive epithet in the contract, but it distinguished the spirit of the company so well that in the scholarly literature it has been frequently treated as a lexicalized name designating the company directed by Maphio Zanini, and hence Fraternal Compagnia is occasionally printed without quotation marks and with upper case initials, like a proper name. Most details specified in the contract concern the management side of the enterprise, covering such things as common ownership of properties, the equal distribution of profits, sick pay and departure from the company. The artistic side of the company's work is expressed in a single rule, which establishes the authority of the company director over all members: they owe him absolute obedience concerning decisions affecting performances and future engagements. By giving the company director this authoritative role, the actors recognized the fact that a performance needed to be sustained by a unifying artistic vision. The same level of authority was enjoyed by the directors of subsequent companies, the most distinguished of which was the company of the Gelosi, directed by Flaminio Scala, which began operations in 1568. The name Gelosi may mean something like jealous guardians of the art that they practised. In general, the self-naming of companies (e.g. Gelosi, Fedeli, Accesi, Uniti) resembles the practice of the literary academies of the time, which aimed to convey their cultural self-understanding by allegorical allusion. In imitation of this practice, the theatre companies chose for themselves names that, at least by analogy, vindicated their role in the development of high culture by arrogating to themselves the not-for-profit attitude of the academies (Tessari 1981–4: 70). Certainly, some of the members of the Gelosi deserve recognition in the world of high culture, reminding us with their work that the entertainment industry and high art are linked by continuity: Flaminio Scala, the Gelosi's first director and leading actor in the role of Flavio, was also a celebrated playwright and the only commedia dell'arte actor in history to publish a collection of scenarios. Francesco Andreini, its second director, was a renowned Capitan Spavento and a writer of no mean reputation. His wife, Isabella Andreini, who rose to diva status like a bright meteor, was also a writer of considerable distinction. The company performed in every major city of Northern Italy and France, in the greatest courts of these countries, raising the artistic profile of the commedia dell'arte and laying the cultural ground for its intersection with local dramatic traditions.

FIGURE 1 *Franken the Elder, Italian actors, the Gelosi troupe with Isabella Andreini in Paris, Musée Carnavalet. (Photo by Photo12/ Universal Images Group via Getty Images)*

From the records of another distinguished company, the one directed by Alberto Naselli, better known by his stage name of Zan Ganassa, we know that company directors could recruit temporary members from the local scene for roles that required special talents, such as knowledge of music. Naselli did such recruiting in Spain, where his company spent most of its active years (Ferrone 2014: 17). From the same records we know that the company had a clearly defined internal organization that enabled it to take care of the business side of its activities with relative ease. In addition to their acting, all members had important non-artistic duties to discharge, such as taking care of costumes and properties, looking after legal problems with local authorities and drafting contracts and agreements for future engagements. The logical distribution of essential labour, in accordance with expertise and inclination, enabled the company to work as a unit.

All these companies represent the commedia dell'arte of Northern Italy. In the south, commedia culture was a little different, and the difference was already visible in the formation of companies. The earliest known legal instrument for the creation of an acting company in Southern Italy, first published by the philosopher Benedetto Croce (Croce 1891: 776–7), is dated 5 July 1575, or thirty years after the establishment of the Northern brotherly company of 1545. The document is a contract by which five actors – Mario de Thomase, Jacobo Antonio de Ferrariis, Alfonso Cortese, Giulio Cesare Farina, Francisco Itiani – agreed to bind themselves into a company for two years for the purpose of 'making and reciting plays' (*il fare et recitare comedie*, Croce 1891: 776) throughout the Kingdom of Naples – which at that time was under Spanish rule and included all of Italy south of the Papal States – and anywhere else in the world where their art might take them. The articles in the contract concern the sharing of profits, sick pay, joint ownership and the like, more or less like those in the contract of the Northern 'fraternal compagnia'.

There are, however, at least three points on which the contract of the Neapolitan company differs significantly from the 1545 document. The first is the distinction between making (*fare*) and reciting (*recitare*) plays, explicitly mentioned as two separate types of activity. The difference may refer, on the one hand, to the art of creating performance texts directly on stage by improvisation, and, on the other hand, to the art of reciting fully scripted plays in the conventional manner. The company, in other words may have performed scripted as well as unscripted plays, and referred to the latter activity using a verb of making, *fare*, in a sense analogous to that of the English *wright* in play*wright*, that is a maker of plays. The second difference is that, in addition to illness as a legitimate ground for compensation without work, the contract adds explicitly that a second circumstance might be imprisonment for an offence due to the activity of the company (*per causa di detta compagnia*). Since in its work as a troupe of players, the company could become the cause of an arrest by the authorities only by asking its players to perform acts of transgression on stage, it is more than likely that the company occasionally expected its performances to appear defiant. The third point concerns female members of the company. Although none of the players that signed the contract was a woman, the contract twice specifically refers to *compagni* and *compagne*, respectively male and female members of the *compagnia* created by the contract.

Women in the companies

Part of the historical importance of the company of Zan Ganassa is the fact that it explicitly listed, for the first time, a woman as a full member of a company. The historical and aesthetic significance of the presence of women in commedia dell'arte companies cannot be overstated. There is no doubt that at first women were welcomed into companies for the erotic appeal that they could give a play, particularly if they were provocatively dressed. Their commodification, observes

Rosalind Kerr, was due to their sex appeal and the illusion of uninhibited availability to which their mere presence on stage gave rise (2015: 7–8). As we shall see in discussing a contemporary theological critique of commedia dell'arte, the misogynists of the age denounced their arrival for their potential to corrupt the young women in the audience and to lead men astray in their own imagination. But the artistic importance of women in the commedia dell'arte was such that a highly respected scholar has gone as far as to say that, prior to the appearance of women on stage, the entire corpus of plays featuring the familiar masked characters in acts of buffoonery can be called commedia dell'arte only by a stretch of the term (Taviani 1982: 338). In the entertainment market of the time, buffoonery (*buffoneria*) was a crude and clownish form of comical entertainment in the proximity of, but in tension with, professional acting, of which it was regarded a spurious variant or '*variante spuria*' (Tessari 2017: 321), prone to expressions of vulgarity in both gesture and language. The arrival of women represented a remarkable change in the aesthetic value of productions, not necessarily because actresses could play female characters with a greater degree of verisimilitude, or because they could give rise to prurience whether they intended to or not, but because women brought into the companies that they joined something that most conventional actors did not have: a liberal education, acquaintance with literature, music, dance and skill in carrying a conversation.

This was certainly the case of the most celebrated actresses of the early commedia dell'arte – Barbara Flaminia, in the first place, since she was the earliest actress whose performances in various cities of Italy and later in Spain, where she had gone with Zan Ganassa, are well documented. She was closely followed by the enormously talented Vincenza Armani, with whom Flaminia competed but also collaborated in Mantua in 1567 and 1568, and the records celebrate them both in superlative terms. Armani could perform in all dramatic genres, sing, play various instruments and compose poetry in both Italian and Latin, skills that she probably acquired in her efforts to gain the approval and regard of powerful members of society (Taviani 1982: 333). In the third place, we find Vittoria Piissimi, who, as prima donna of the Gelosi, probably played the role of Silvia in a much celebrated production of TorquatoTasso's *Aminta* in the summer court theatre of the Duke of Ferrara in 1573. Vittoria had the fortune and misfortune of being much admired by possessive dukes of Modena and Mantova as well as Ferrara and frequently found herself having to adapt her professional trajectory to their requests. Throughout her career, she was in great demand, and she performed with the most celebrated companies of the time, including the Confidenti and the Uniti but mostly with the Gelosi.

Finally comes Isabella Andreini, a star more dazzling than all the great actresses that preceded her in the commedia dell'arte. She joined the Gelosi at age fourteen together with her husband Francesco Andreini, playing the maidservant next to Vittoria Piissimi as the leading lady (the *Prima Amorosa*), but she took over that role when Vittoria left the Gelosi to join the Confidenti. Isabella rose quickly to great fame, and her personal life was so closely associated with her stage life that she is generally recognized as the first real diva of the European stage. Regarded as supremely beautiful and hugely talented, Isabella achieved great success and lent much lustre to the already distinguished company of the Gelosi, which thrived under the direction of her husband. She was celebrated by poets as an actress, a poetess and a woman of great virtue. She died unexpectedly while the Gelosi were touring France; Francesco was so heartbroken that he dissolved the company and stopped acting, dedicating himself for some time to the publication of her works and the consolidation of her fame.

These stars of the early commedia dell'arte were working women who had managed to acquire the right cultural background to pursue employment in the entertainment industry, where they could market their talent. We know very little of their origin, though, on the basis of contemporary accounts, we can surmise that, despite their generally humble birth, they managed to acquire skills similar to those of cultured courtesans who could offer noblemen the solace of literary conversation and graceful manners as part of their companionship. The skills of early professional actresses resemble those of women then known as *meretrices honestae* or honest courtesans (Taviani 1982: 333–5). Unlike the actors who preceded them in the profession, men who marketed their ability to perform technically demanding but uncouth acts of buffoonery, the women brought refinement to the companies that they joined. Their acquaintance with literature and their conversational skills made them especially talented improvisers of refined speech. The amalgamation of the cultural urbanity of the women and the mimetic skill of the men changed the ethos of early companies, giving them almost immediately much more ambitious artistic goals to pursue, some of which were clearly visible in company repertoires.

The company repertoire

In considering the repertoire of a commedia dell'arte company, it is essential to keep in mind a basic premise: the company could not survive long without a methodic repertoire-development practice. Typically, the creative work of the composition process was divided into two different stages and involved a clear distribution of labour. The work of the first stage was the responsibility of a playwright, who could very well also be an actor, and consisted of the conception of a dramatic action and its arrangement into a plot. The product of this part of the composition preceded the performance and was called either a *soggetto* (subject) or a *canovaccio* (canvas) or more commonly a *scenario,* which could be either an original conception or a story derived from an existing literary work. The creative work of the second stage fell to the players in the cast and consisted of the composition of the actual words and gestures of the performance, and this part was accomplished directly on stage by improvisation and memory (Taviani 1982: 377). In the performance text, that is the play as perceived by the audience, the two stages appeared materialized into a single activity. The distinction between the two stages of the composition process, however, is basic to any understanding of how companies could build up a large repertoire of plays for production with minimal or no preparation time. The repertoire was what enabled them to remain competitive in the entertainment market.

The repertoire of individual companies included not only scenarios but also fully scripted plays, to be performed either in the conventional manner or by an improvisatory rendering of the original. Many excellent plays were composed by actors. Giambattista Andreini, for example, wrote some of the very best Italian plays of the seventeenth century. Whether it was as writers or as improvisatory players, all the members of a company needed an excellent grounding in literature, and needed to read assiduously and commit to memory as many stories, plays and speeches as possible. Scenario writers prepared themselves to recall at will plots and episodes, while players trained themselves to recall speeches on which to model their own creations in the appropriate stylistic register. The proximity between the scripted and unscripted repertoire of the commedia dell'arte troupes led to the writing of numerous plays which employ the same masked characters of the unscripted tradition. The only difference is that in one case we have only a scenario, and in the other a full script, but both are essentially commedia forms. The more inclusive the repertoire, the more successful the company could be, at least in theory. A large repertoire had great economic advantages, since the company could produce other plays on short notice and keep a good calendar of engagements. It is especially when we consider the repertoire of a company that we realize just how closely the commedia dell'arte is related to the literary canon of classical, near-contemporary and contemporary drama, Italian as well as foreign.

Whereas the repertoire of individual actors consisted of speeches and expressions peculiar to particular parts, the repertoire of a company consisted mostly of scenarios. We shall have more to say about the relationship between the scenario form and the actors' creation of a performance text in a later chapter, but for the moment it is sufficient to note that the writers in the company had developed a formula for composing them very quickly. This convention enabled the actors to produce a performance text with little preparation. The performance text of a scenario was largely an assemblage of previously memorized pieces from different sources reproduced in the actors' own words.

In a competitive market, the composition of a scenario itself and its dramaturgical preparation for performance had at times to be accomplished very quickly. One way of doing this was to acquire a repertoire of scenes and episodes that could be used in different dramaturgical designs of the same action and could hence be included in a variety of plays. Scenes invested with this function might include dialogues based on a mistaken identity, the appearance of a ghost, the discovery that a character believed dead is actually alive or the realization that one is sleeping with the wrong lover, and the like. Cesare Molinari has persuasively argued that scenario writers had at their disposal a repertory of such scenes, all scenes of proven success, which they could include in a number of different plots, more or less the way Renaissance fresco artists used the same cartoons to paint similar figures and poses in wall paintings with a different theme and narrative (Molinari 1997: 24–5).

This approach to scenario composition and dramaturgical organization enabled companies to stage a play very quickly, combining new materials with recycled functional scenes of varying complexity. Ideally one could place at one end of a spectrum a scenario with a large number of such recycled scenes and at the other end a scenario with very few or no recognizable scenes of this type. The repertory-heavy scenario could be interpreted as aimed at actor-centred performances, which is to say performances whose dramaturgical design made greater use of virtuosic stage business than the plot itself, while a repertory-light scenario could be seen as aimed at playwright conditioned performances in the manner of a scripted literary comedy with a greater claim to authorial authorship and originality.

2

Elements of form:

Characters and dramatic actions

Early in the history of their professionalization, commedia dell'arte actors began to develop their art around a very simple concept of dramatic form, understood as a set of plot-building conventions and character relations that could be used to generate the skeletal structure of plays in genres as different as pastoral tragicomedy and unscripted farce. Such a skeletal structure could be regarded as 'the lowest common multiple', as Siro Ferrone has aptly described it, of all the plays available to a company (1985: 11). Differently stated, the underlying dramatic form of a company's repertoire is a matrix of characters and dramatic actions that could be used to generate a large variety of performances by a series of permutations and commutations, requiring only the addition of a few thematic elements to foreground the uniqueness of a specific play. Such a matrix could give a company the versatility to perform plays of different kinds and a base on which to build a large and diversified repertoire. The trick was to make the set of skills in the company compatible with the matrix.

Company organization and the dramaturgy of action

At the most basic level, the dramatic action of a romantic pursuit – the preferred theme of comedy – shows how lovers overcome obstacles to their union. From an organizational point of view, this means that a skeletal company would need two players for the parts of the lovers, generically known as the *Amoroso* and the *Amorosa,* two players in the role of the obstacle-generating fathers, known as the *vecchi*, and one or two servants, conventionally called *zanni,* to help the lovers overcome the difficulties they encountered with stratagems that would keep the plot moving, and, finally, a maid, the *servetta*, as the lady's helper and confidante. Other characters were occasionally added to create intrigue and regional colour, the latter usually in minor roles. The minimal composition of an acting troupe pursuing a repertoire based on this matrix would have to include at least six players, each in possession of a collection of parts that could be reused in different plots articulated by improvisation. This was in fact the main scheme for the organization of companies in Northern Italy. In the South, the principle of organization was different.

To understand the difference between Northern and Southern commedia dell'arte, it is necessary to distinguish clearly between *type* and *character.* By character we mean an individual in a particular play, whereas by type we mean a group of characters who are essentially variants of each other, that is, who belong to the same type (Bragaglia 1959: 6; Molinari 1985). Thus, for example, Truffaldino, the protagonist of Goldoni's *Servant of Two Masters,* is a specific character; the type to which he belongs is that of the second *zanni,* or the type of Arlecchino or Harlequin in English, Truffaldino being only a version of Harlequin. A poem by Giovan Maria Rapparini from 1718 lists twenty-four characters of the same type as Harlequin (Oreglia 1968: 64). Each of these characters is slightly different from the others but sufficiently close to them to be regarded as an embodiment of the same type, the type of the servant whose behaviour oscillates between cleverness and foolishness. In Northern commedia dell'arte, acting troupes were organized by type, with at least one actor specialized in a character of each type. If an actor left the company, a replacement was sought among the pool of actors who specialized in the type left vacant by the departing actor. The incoming actor would be expected to play a variation of the character previously played by his predecessor. The variations themselves were created by individual actors by developing some aspects of the type in a way that reflected their particular talent and professional self-understanding, frequently giving the character a different name. This was not generally the case in the South. Pulcinella, for example, was not regarded as the representative of a type that could include many different variations of the same character all cast in the same role. He is rather a specific character, who could be encountered in roles of radically different kinds. It is true that we meet him most frequently in the role of a servant, but he could just as easily be in that of an ageing father, a young lover or a prince. In all these roles he would exhibit the defining features of Pulcinella's character and could not be mistaken for anybody else. Whereas in Northern commedia dell'arte, the role of a character in a particular play is a function of the type to which the character belongs, in the Southern version the role is largely a function of the specific character who, in that play, happens to have a role of that type. Troupes in the South tended to be organized largely by character specialization, the actor being expected to perform the same character in roles of different types, depending on the play.

When we think of commedia dell'arte, we tend to think of its characters rather than the stories in which they appear. This is because generations of skilled actors impersonating their roles, together with the iconography that they generated in the decorative arts, have crystallized them in the popular imagination and have given them an existence comparable to that of mythological figures. We might be tempted to assume that the stories were composed, whether in scripted or in unscripted form, to make the characters come to life and to reveal things about them that the audience did not know at the beginning of the play. But that was not the case.

In the commedia dell'arte the relationship between character and action was conceived along conventional classical terms (Taviani 1982: 329). To the dramaturgical question whether, in the construction of a play, the action could be regarded as a function of the characters' behaviour, or vice versa, the classical view was that characters were always a function of the action, and were always conceived only as its agents, for the action was the only truly indispensable ingredient of drama, as Aristotle observed (*Poetics* 1450a). The dramatic action, and hence the plot in which it was arranged, preceded everything else, ontologically as well as chronologically.

In the commedia dell'arte, the stories, frequently adapted from the literary tradition, dramatic and otherwise, preceded the stage life of the characters and were reorganized as a scenario for production, and they were not to be changed in performance. The behaviour and the dialogue of characters could be entrusted to the creativity of individual performers, but not the dramatic action itself, which was the play's starting condition. The action was not a device for the progressive revelation of character in a succession of episodes, because the plays were not about the secret inner life of characters. Commedia characters had no inner life to speak of. They were what they appeared to be. The dramatic action provided the performers with a context in which they could display their art in bringing the characters to life, which they did by transforming the dramatic action into speech and stage business of their creation, in accordance with the nature of the action.

The principal characters

In examining the principal characters of a commedia dell'arte play – in the Northern as well as in the Southern variety – it is useful to distinguish two layers of meaning that could be perceived by the audience. In the first layer, the characters figured only in their actantial function, and hence as key elements of its dramatic form. In this sense, the principal characters were ready-made for both the author and the actors as part of the basic material used to create a play. In the course of a play, they were doers and receivers of actions, but they did not undergo any significant development. The changes that they did experience were changes in situation rather than personality, changes that might cause them to exhibit some of their defining features more than others, but such changes did not bring about the emergence of new defining features. Their identifying features were found in the performance tradition and in visual representations that preceded the play in question. Since the characters were familiar, there was a large quantity of information that the audience could be assumed to have about them before the play actually began. Thus, the audience's familiarity with Harlequin or Pulcinella, for example, was one of the starting conditions of any play in which their names might appear among the dramatis personae.

In the second layer of meaning, the characters figured as a function of the style and skill of the particular performers who impersonated them. In this sense, the characters reflected the uniqueness imparted to the familiar role by the actors in the course of the performance. By the end of the play, the audience's expectations, generated in them by their acquaintance with tradition, were both confirmed and enriched in all the special ways that were within the performers' technical abilities. Borrowing two terms from the linguistics of information, we might call the already familiar and the freshly acquired information about characters their *givenness* and *newness* (Gundel and Fretheim 2009: 147–9). The performance can then be regarded as a dynamic interface between the givenness and newness of each character.

In the semiotic practice of the commedia dell'arte, the givenness of its principal characters consisted of the aggregate of signs by which the audience could identify them upon first encounter, namely the costumes they wore, the regional dialect

they spoke, their typical stage activities and their agentive role in
the unfolding of the action. These were the chief stage markers
of the characters' identity. Each marker came with a wealth
of associations and raised specific expectations of behaviour.
Newness, on the other hand, consisted of the set of more or less
subtle variations injected by the actor, in a particular performance,
into the audience's idea of what the character was like and what
they expected him to do in the play. Newness is the special colour
added by the actor to the markings of the character's semiotic
givenness. At the core of every moment of the performance
there was a dialectic interplay between the formal givenness of
a character, invariable in both essence and appearance, and the
newness, resulting from the creativity of the performer striving to
inform the stage life of the character with the distinctiveness of
his or her real temperament as a player (Andrews 1993: 173) or
of his or her constructed persona as a performer.

Throughout the performance and at the end of the play,
the result of this dialectic was a character exhibiting both the
invariable traits of his conventional givenness and the freshness
of the actor's stage personality. The action was designed to
allow characters with fixed and well-known traits to function
as its credible agents, and to make it possible for the actors
to infuse into those traits the distinctiveness of their personal
performance styles. The success of the play depended very much
on the characters' liveliness on stage, on their antics and on the
ability of the actors impersonating them to improvise speeches
and behaviour that could personalize them somewhat – that
is, that could confer on them the distinctiveness of the actors
themselves – while displaying the traits by which the characters
were known in the received tradition.

At each stage of the history of commedia dell'arte, the array
of characters that could be engaged in new creative work was
not vast. It is true that, from the sixteenth century on, commedia
dell'arte actors embodied a very large variety of characters, each
with its recognizable givenness, but only a few of them actually
survived long periods of history and became known beyond
their immediate region or city of origin. Gianduja and his wife

Giacometta from Piedmont, Meneghino and his wife Cecca from Lombardy, Stenterello and Burlamacco from Florence, Pasquino from Sicily, Bertuccio from Umbria, Turchetta the slave girl from Naples – none of these managed to transcend the geographical boundaries of their origin and qualify as canonical characters of mainstream performances in other areas of Italy. Similarly, Burattino and Pedrolino, the latter the original Pierrot, suffered from analogous limitations. These are only a few examples of the large number of cheerful characters that appeared in commedia dell'arte plays. Some of them flourished in particular periods of history but later dropped out of popularity, despite their occasional re-emergence on stage in the company of more established characters.

The following paragraphs provide a synoptic view of the established characters, listed with their identifying traits. The first group includes the characters prevalent in Northern Italy; the second, those found chiefly in the South.

Northern characters

The Amoroso and Amorosa are respectively a young man and a young woman in love. Their costumes are stylish contemporary dress, their manner of movement is refined and their speech is always elegant, even in passages of quick dialogue, in stark contrast with all other stock characters of the commedia dell'arte. They speak Tuscan, as the literary language of Italy was still called, and their stylistic register is high, informed by the rhetoric of love poetry. By their style and language, the lovers represent the most conspicuous imbrication of the commedia dell'arte in the national literary tradition of Italy. In his treatise on acting, Andrea Perrucci (2008 [1699]) observed that, in addition to mastering appropriate physical and vocal performance techniques, all actors specializing in the roles of the lovers were required to have an excellent background in literature, rhetoric and grammar (Ferrone 2014: 243; Perrucci 2008 [1699]: 163)

The Dottore is an old academic, a pedant from Bologna, seat of the oldest university in Italy. Consistently with his origins, he speaks a dialect from the region of Emilia Romagna, most notably Bolognese. Since this dialect is rather difficult to understand in other regions of Italy, in cities far from Bologna the performer would have to make his vernacular more intelligible by bringing it closer to Tuscan, of which many people had a passive knowledge. In any case, the Dottore's speech was untidily strewn with comical malapropisms and cacologies. His dialogues and monologues are marked by frequent instances of comical code-switching, as he was in the habit of injecting into his Bolognese all manner of phrases in macaronic Latin, in which vernacular words were inflected to sound like Latin and yet be recognizable as vernacular

HABIT DE DOCTEUR MODERNE

FIGURE 2 *Dottore, engraving from Luigi Riccoboni (1676–1731),* Histoire du théâtre italien, *Paris, 1728 (via Wikimedia Commons, public domain).*

parlance. The purpose of such code-switching was to offer a parody of juridical Latin, since the Dottore's 'doctorate' was originally in law (Ferrone 2014: 247).

Pantalone evolved into an old merchant from Venice from an earlier character known as the Magnifico. Pantalone was emblematic of his native city, whose mercantile power dominated the Mediterranean. Pantalone spoke only Venetian and was distinguished by comical as well as serious traits. His comical nature derives in part from his costume – tight-fitting red trousers and shirt, with a black cloak and a mask with a hooked nose – and from his unbecoming behaviour when he yields to his lecherous imagination. His serious aspects derives instead from his social status as a successful business man, though he is always ungenerous and protective of his riches.

FIGURE 3 *Pantalone, engraving from a drawing by Maurice Sand (1823–89) in* Masques et bouffons, comédie Italienne, *Paris, 1860. (Photo by DeAgostini/Getty Images.)*

Pantalone and Dottore are the two *vecchi* or the old men of commedia plots.

Brighella and Harlequin are servants originally from the city of Bergamo, located in a distant and depressed region of the Republic of Venice. In Venice itself, they are immigrants who speak either their dialect of origin, Bergamask, or Venetian with a heavy Bergamask accent. They both evolved from the earlier character known as a *zanni*, the trickster servant, who was central to the commedia dell'arte conception of comedy in the early decades of its history. Brighella, who is also known as the first *zanni*, is the cleverer of the two and is prone, as the etymology of his name suggests, to cause trouble ('briga'). He wears a black mask and the livery of a well-to-do house

FIGURE 4 *Harlequin in 1671, illustrated by Maurice Sand (1823–89), engraving from* Masques et bouffons, comédie Italienne, *Paris, 1860. France, nineteenth century. Venice, Casa Di Carlo Goldoni. (Photo by DeAgostini/Getty Images.)*

consisting of white trousers and short jacket with green stripes along the sides. Harlequin's costume consists of shirt and trousers covered with colourful patches, to indicate his poverty, though in time the patches became stylized geometric figures without a real referent.

The servetta or woman servant was the Amorosa's maid and hence an aide and confidante in her romantic pursuits. Known by various names, including Colombina (little dove), Corallina (little coral) and Smeraldina (little emerald), which are her most famous names, the servetta was a young working woman with a highly developed libido, a soubrette predisposed to marriage with the likes of Harlequin in subplots mirroring the love story of the main characters. Her costume was a simple working-class dress with a waist apron. The role of the servetta occasionally included dancing and singing.

The Capitano is a braggart soldier always prone to fustian speech and expressions of narcissism about his heroic exploits and his appearance. A caricature of the foreign military forces in Italy, chiefly the Spanish army in the Southern regions, but also German soldiers in Northern Italy. He spoke a language consisting of a Southern dialect – usually Neapolitan or Sicilian – and Spanish, though when he appears on Northern stages, the foreign component of his language is frequently German. He wears a colourful and flamboyant uniform with a very long sword.

Southern characters

Pulcinella is easily the most famous character in the commedia dell'arte, with a virtually uninterrupted performance tradition in and around Naples. His name is a diminutive of *pulcino* or chick, perhaps an allusion to the fact that his hump-shaped torso and pot belly suggested the profile of a chicken. He was frequently paired with Zeza, the Neapolitan diminutive of Lucrezia, who was his mistress or his wife. He spoke the

FIGURE 5 *Pulcinella, from* The Humour of Italy, *Internet Archive book image (via Wikimedia Commons, public domain).*

Neapolitan dialect and, in the popular imagination, became a symbol of Naples itself. Whatever role he may have been cast in, Pulcinella exhibited the same traits. He could be witless or sharp-witted, as the occasion demanded, but he was generally awkward and always hungry. He wore wide trousers and a long baggy shirt, both white, with a black mask and a sugar-cone hat, though the hat changed shape various times since the early seventeenth century.

Giangurgolo was a character representative of the region of Calabria, whose dialect he spoke. In Calabrian his name means one who gorges himself greedily to satisfy hunger or gluttony. Giangurgolo wore a long-nosed mask with a colourful costume consisting of paned breeches and a slashed doublet with paned sleeves and a wide collar. Like Pulcinella and other Southern

FIGURE 6 *Giangurgolo in 1625, engraving from an illustration by Maurice Sand (1823–89) in* Masques et bouffons, comédie Italienne, Paris, 1860. Venice, Casa Di Carlo Goldoni. *(Photo by DeAgostini/ Getty Images.)*

characters, he could be found in many roles: he could play the father, the son, the servant, the lover and the Capitano. When he was in the role of the Capitano, he infused his Calabrian dialect with Spanish or Spanish-sounding expressions (Bragaglia 1959: 4).

Coviello was the Southern equivalent of the Northern *zanni* (Bragaglia 1959: 4). Though he could be considered a native of any region of Southern Italy, he was most frequently identified as Sicilian, and in that dialect his name is a diminutive of Jacovo. He was generally depicted in a hose-like bodysuit with a plumed hat, dancing and playing a mandolin or other small string instrument. He spoke the dialect of the region with which he was identified and hence

FIGURE 7 *Coviello, engraving from an illustration by Maurice Sand (1823–89) in* Masques et bouffons, comédie Italienne, *Paris, 1860 (via Wikimedia Commons, public domain).*

most frequently Sicilian. He was acrobatic and could be either foolish or clever though always freewheeling. Like various other Southern characters, he could be cast in different roles, though he was most often a servant. In scenarios from different parts of Italy, he might also appear as a merchant or a gentleman (Castagno 1994: 87).

Tartaglia was a character linked to various Southern regions, most notably Campania and Calabria. He wore a mask with large spectacles and was generally depicted in breeches and doublet with bright yellow and green horizontal stripes. In addition to poor eyesight, Tartaglia had a natural speech impediment that caused him to stutter constantly. As is suggested by his name, which means 'the stutterer', stuttering was his chief identifying trait. He had difficulty pronouncing all consonants, especially the 'r' (Perrucci 2008 [1699]: 144). He spoke a Southern dialect, though, as Perrucci surmised, the role could be played equally well in any language. The actor impersonating him, however, could not rely only on the comic effect of mispronounced words and repeated syllables but needed to convey and render comical the physical effort and momentary convulsion of a person striving to overcome a natural defect, which the actor had to do wearing a mask.

Scaramuccia, better known as Scaramouche, the French version of his name, was originally a Neapolitan variant of the Capitano. A notorious womanizer and a hard drinker, Scaramuccia was a dark and quarrelsome character whose

FIGURE 8 *Scaramouche, engraving from Luigi Riccoboni (1676–1731),* Histoire du théâtre italien, *Paris 1728 (via Wikimedia Commons, public domain).*

behaviour could be generally explained by reference to his nefarious motives. His nature was reflected in his name, which means 'skirmish'. He wore breeches, a doublet and a cap, all black. At first, he was expected to make grimaces with his face and hence did not wear a mask, but in the course of the seventeenth century, he added a black mask to his costume and altered his performance style accordingly.

Costumes and masks

The actors playing the lovers and the maid appeared in typical contemporary dress, costumes that signified their gender and social class. In this respect the production of a commedia dell'arte play was similar to that of most other European staged plays, in which, until approximately the end of the eighteenth century, non-allegorical characters were dressed in contemporary clothes, without a mask. The actors representing the other characters wore costumes which originally symbolized social condition (the poverty of Harlequin) and occupation (the Dottore's academic gown). But this signifying function was eventually lost, and the costumes served only to identify the characters and to locate them in a horizon of expected behaviour for the audience (Molinari and Ottolenghi 1985: 94). The costumes of the lovers signified by visual resemblance the society to which they belonged. They were visual metonymies or figures of contiguity. They could stand alongside off-stage clothes as elements of the same fashion universe. The costumes of the masked characters, on the other hand, signified by visual difference their discontinuity with society, in which no real set of clothing resembled them directly. Such costumes were visual metaphors or figures of substitution. Next to off-stage clothes they signified, in the first place, the theatrical identity of those who wore them, and, in the second place, artificially constructed social types and their typical behaviour. They did, however, signify metonymically when considered next to the costumes of carnival pageantry, itself a form of ritualistic theatricality in which the masked characters of the commedia dell'arte had leading roles throughout Italy, next to a large number of other costumed characters that never acquired a profile of note in actual theatres.

In discussions of the commedia dell'arte, the word 'mask' has three different meanings. Its first sense is related to acting, in the context of which it designates the face-covering that we call by that name in English. Commedia masks, which generally covered only the upper half of the face, were worn by actors when they played certain characters. It is in this sense that we use the term when we speak of masked performance conventions. In its second sense, masks, most commonly in the plural, is a generic name for the masked characters themselves: Harlequin, Pantalone, Brighella, Pulcinella and Dottore are the principal masks of the commedia dell'arte tradition, that is, its main masked characters. In the third sense, its meaning was expanded to cover all commedia dell'arte characters, including the ones that did not normally appear with a mask, though in this sense the term occurs less frequently than in the other two.

Masks constitute the facial part of a costume. In the commedia dell'arte tradition masks were generally made of leather, which was regarded as superior to papier mâché, the other commonly used material. The higher desirability of leather masks is due especially to the suppleness of the material, which gave masks a wider range of expressiveness, was easier to shape for a comfortable fit, and lasted a relatively long time. Commedia dell'arte masks evolved into a variety of shapes, but since the early years of its history, when Harlequin's mask could cover his entire face, they were typically half-masks, covering the face from the forehead to the upper lip, though some masks, like that of Tartaglia which was shaped like large spectacles, left most of the face exposed. Two points of great interest in mask design were the size of the eyeholes, which could vary from small to large, and their basic shape, which could be circular, nephroidal or almond-like. The size of the opening had biomechanical implications, particularly when they were circular. For example, early masks of Harlequin and Pulcinella had very small circular eyeholes which greatly reduced the actor's lateral vision in a tunnel-like manner. An excellent illustration is the portrait of the actor Tommaso Antonio Visentini, also known as Thomassin, who played Harlequin with great distinction in Lelio Riccoboni's company in Paris, holding his mask in his right hand close enough to his face (Taviani and Schino 1982: 26) for us to be able to assess the size of the eyeholes by a simple comparison: the eyeholes of the mask are smaller than the irises of his eyes.

The lack of lateral vision forced the actor to make quick angular movements with his head and, by extension, with his arms and legs, in response to speech from other characters or in order to move forward. This manner of movement gave his performance style a mechanical appearance, almost as if the character being portrayed were a hybrid of puppet and human. William Hogarth, who was a keen observer of the performance style of commedia dell'arte players, observed that the actors performing Pulcinella generally had to move as if their limbs were joined to their bodies by hinges, because that was what was required to portray the character. For analogous reasons, actors who played Harlequin had to move as if they were always shooting straight lines from their limbs into the surrounding air and twirling circles about their heads (Hogarth 1753: 143), because that was the movement style of their character.

Together with their lateral dimension, the shape of the eyeholes also influenced the audience's perception of the personality of the character as portrayed by a given actor. In modern times, Sear Eldredge experimented with lima-bean shaped (nephroidal) and cat-like shaped (upturned almond) eyeholes for Truffaldino's mask in a production of Goldoni's *The Servant of Two Masters*. He found that a mask with cat-like eyeholes created the impression that Truffaldino was 'a conniving, scheming manipulator', with little to endear him to the audience, whereas the same mask with bean-like eyes turned him into 'a bumbling innocent who fell into solutions rather than one who planned them' (Eldredge 1996: 172). These two examples, one historical the other modern, illustrate the crucial role played by mask design details in the actor's transformation of his body into a clear signifying structure. As we shall see in the last chapter, the distinguished actor Marcello Moretti, who gave the figure of Harlequin renewed currency under the direction of Giorgio Strehler at the Piccolo Teatro di Milano, preferred a mask with feline eyeholes for much the same reasons. The mask's eyeholes are linked in an indissoluble way to the rest of the actor's costume and contribute to both the form of his personal performance style and the perspective of the audience's hermeneutical approach to the character's role in the performance text.

3

Elements of form:

The scenario, improvisation and *lazzi*

With his publication of il *teatro delle favole rappresentative* (1611), Flaminio Scala tried to bring the concept of an unscripted play into the domain of literature, possibly on the understanding that scenarios could also be regarded as literary works worthy of being read. Most scenarios written before and after Scala's were meant only for performers and not for the general reader, more or less the way musical scores are meant only for those who have the technical skill to read them, and so they were generally not printed. Scala must have thought that, with a little effort, he could present his scenarios to a public larger than the handful of players who would otherwise profit from them. To this effect he modified the usual scenario form in order to make it accessible to non-actors, adding an Argomento, a term of rhetorical origin that by the sixteenth century was commonly used to denote the summary of a play and its essential background (Herrick 1964: 93). Such summaries would be hardly necessary if the scenarios were meant only for actors. They are certainly missing from most other scenarios in the tradition. Scala also organized his collection as if the scenarios were tales of some sort, distributing them into fifty days, ultimately on the example of Boccaccio's *Decameron*, which consisted of one hundred tales to be told in ten days.

But scenarios are not tales, and they are notoriously difficult to read without some knowledge of the theatre culture in which they were written. Unlike tales and scripted plays, which are relatively easy to read, scenarios are only an element of dramatic form, the other textual components of which are speech and gesture, which are only implied in the scenarios but are left for the actor to produce. The performance text was generated by the players, observing the thematic restrictions and narrative logic of the scenario. They gave a material body to the dramatic action in the scenario, adding in the process comic business of their own in the form of physical and verbal routines, both clever and demanding, known as *lazzi*.

Accordingly, this chapter examines the scenario, understood as a complex system of promptings for the creation of a performance text directly on stage; improvisation, as the technique for monologue and dialogue creation, both verbal and gestural; and *lazzi,* or the virtuosic comic routines of the performers, strategically deployed in scenarios to give them brilliance and aesthetic appeal as performance texts.

The dramatic action

Among the scenarios in Flaminio Scala's *Il teatro delle favole rappresentative* (1611), *Il marito* occupies a privileged space in the history of the commedia dell'arte because it was later turned by Scala into a fully scripted play, called *Il finto marito* (1618), with two dialogic prologues. In the first of these, the author, imagining a conversation between an actor (*Comico*) and a foreigner (*Forestiero*) speaking about a performance, proposes a poetics of unscripted drama. The actor defends the art of making plays directly on stage without a script against severe criticism from the foreigner. The actor argues vigorously that action and not language constitutes the indissoluble part of dramatic form. Predictably, his argument presupposes a mimetic concept of drama, ultimately derived from Aristotle's *Poetics,* according to which drama is fundamentally the imitation of an action.

The sentence on which Scala hinges his concept of an unscripted play has an unusually technical ring: 'le commedie nell'azzioni consistono propriamente et in sustanzia, e nelle narrazioni per accidente' (Scala, I, cxiii). Frequently quoted by theatre scholars, this definition has been variously interpreted. The reading proposed here is based on the recognition that the words used by Scala to explain the concept of action belong to the analytical terminology of Renaissance Aristotelianism and Scholasticism. It does not take much intimacy with the philosophical culture of the time to recognize the fact that Scala is borrowing technical language from metaphysics to give his definition of a successful play as seen in a performance. Substance and accident are the traditional categories used to explain the concept of being and related ideas, such as the essences of things and all their properties. Scala's use of these terms links his definition of an improvised play, perceived only as a performance text, to the high culture of his age, in which the substance–accident discourse played a role of considerable importance for various disciplines, including logic, metaphysics and theology. Since Scala could have easily used less technical language to say the same thing, the fact that he resorted to this vocabulary is very interesting. For Scala sought to give the art of unscripted drama the profile of a creative activity worthy of recognition by the highest culture of his time, with which he implicitly claimed it had in common the gravity of serious philosophical thought.

The fact that Scala's definition of comedy is spoken by a *comico*, that is an actor, is meant to be taken as a sign that contemporary commedia players are not as unschooled as the levity of the comic stage might suggest, but educated men and women with the highest cultural ambition for their art. Like all other things, comedies consist of a substance, or the prime matter out of which they are fashioned and without which they would have no existence. This substance has accidents, or properties that inhere in it, without being themselves the ontological base of its existence. Comedies, says Scala, consist of actions (*nell'azzioni consistono*) and explains that their consistence is understood both in logical terms (*propriamente,* 'properly') and in metaphysical terms (*in sustanzia,* 'in substance'). In the performance text, plays may also be said to consist of verbal discourse (*e nelle narrazioni,* 'and in expositions'), though the verbal stuff of dialogues and monologues may be identified with a play only attributively (*per accidente*) rather than substantively (*in sustantia*), because the words themselves, whether scripted or improvised, do not constitute its essence.

In the performance text of a comedy, as in all other things, substance and accidents are joined together, though they are not equally important to its existence. A play is the imitation of an action, of which dialogue and monologues are no more than a manifestation of that imitation as verbal performance. Scala calls the linguistic dimension of plays *narrazioni*, adapting for his purposes the plural form of the Latin *narratio,* a term borrowed from courtroom rhetoric, where it designated a verbal account of the facts of a case. Scala's predecessors in this linguistic borrowing were the Latin Renaissance commentators of Terence, who used the term to indicate an exposition of the action of the play (Herrick 1964: 29). Clearly *narrazioni* are things predicated of actions, which, in addition to such properties (accidents) as length and unity, also have a verbal expression. The *narrazioni* of an unscripted play, such as any of Scala's own, are the attributes through which the dramatic action invented by the author of the scenario receives an articulation as verbal performance on stage. There could be no performance *narrazioni* worthy of the name without a previously conceived dramatic action.

The scenario

Although the antics of the stock characters are what we remember best of a commedia dell'arte performance, there can be no doubt that the foundation of a play is the scenario, in which the dramatic action is given in full. Commonly also known in Italian as a *canovaccio*, the scenario has the appearance of a play whose action has been reduced to a long set of stage directions implying the types of activities the actors should perform to give it verbal and physical materiality on stage. The dialogues and monologues are left for the performer to compose directly on stage by improvisation. The scenario is at once a concise outline of the plot and a set of instructions for the actors on how to develop it in performance.

A glance at the extant scenarios is sufficient for us to understand that the commedia dell'arte covered all genres, from comedy to tragedy, although it soon became dominated by comedy. Heck's census of commedia dell'arte scenarios lists 820 titles (Heck 1988), though the suggestion has been made that in the known manuscript collections there may be as many as one thousand (Cuppone 2001: 121, 136–9). The scenarios can be grouped in a variety of ways in order to help the reader grasp patterns and trends over relatively long periods of time. One very useful classification would be to group them according to the relationship between scripted and unscripted drama by which they are informed. Accordingly, the scenarios fall into one of four categories: i) scenarios that have come down to us only in that form, which is to say the vast majority of the scenarios in all known collections; ii) scenarios that, once performed on stage by improvisation, were turned into fully scripted plays, such as Flaminio Scala's *Il finto marito* iii) scenarios derived from scripted plays and produced by improvisation by players familiar with the original text, such as Giambattista Della Porta's *La trappolaria,* which was derived from Plautus' *Pseudolus*, and the anonymous *Il convitato di pietra,* derived from Tirso de Molina's *El burlador de Sevilla;*

and iv) scenarios that include scenes of scripted dialogue to be committed to memory by the actors, famous examples of which are Goldoni's *Momolo cortesan* and Carlo Gozzi's *Turandot*.

An advantage of this classification is that it enables us to see by simple inspection that there was a strong connection between the unscripted and the scripted traditions, which continued to nourish each other in both Northern and Southern commedia dell'arte. A second advantage is that it enables us to assess, again by simple inspection, what type of dramaturgy is required in the preparation of a performance text. Scenarios in the first category place the dramaturgical burden on the players themselves and on the actor selected to exercise the role of dramaturg, namely the company's *concertatore* (Pietropaolo 2006: 93–4; Perrucci 2008 [1699]: 193), who determines the logic of the production in view of its intended impact on the audience. The second category requires a dramaturgy grounded also in the text of the scripted version, since that is likely to govern the interpretation of the scenario for scholars and general audience alike. The dramaturgy of the third category must take into account the recent reception history of the pre-existing scripted play, since that may well represent the paradigm of stage interpretation through which the audience is likely to view the performance. The fourth category involves not only the performance dramaturgy of the first group, which allows a considerable degree of manipulation of the elements of performance, but also a narrower text-based dramaturgy, since the verbal part of some scenes is fixed while the rest is completely open to improvisation.

In order to facilitate the improvisation of the performance text of a scenario in any of these categories without spending much time on dramaturgical preparation, the scenarios were frequently written in such a way as to allow the performers to insert generic repertory pieces at certain points of the plot. Such pieces could include not only short bits of business, such as weeping with accompanying lament, but monologues of some consistency already committed to memory, so long as they did not introduce illogicalities into the plot. Such pieces are functionally a little like the arias known in opera as suitcase arias (*arie di baule*), that is to say arias in a singer's repertoire that could be used in various librettos to save the singer the work of learning a new one each time. In a commedia dell'arte scenario, the places where such integrations can take place, which, since Robert Henke introduced the term, have come to be called 'insertion points' (Henke 2002: 120), may have been spotted by simple inspection of a scenario by the actors, but can be identified by modern scholars only from careful and comparative analysis. In his annotated translation of a selection of Scala's scenarios, Richard Andrews has shown just how numerous these insertion points actually are (2008: 16–18), so numerous in fact that they may be said to constitute an essential feature of the scenario form as understood by Scala.

Unusual instead are instructions to the actors on precisely how to perform a given action on stage. In scene 2.15 of Scala's *The Two Old Twins,* the actor in the role of the slave is instructed to keep out of the other actors' line of sight while on stage, so that he can emerge all at once, as if conjured up by magic, when his character's name is mentioned by the actress playing Pasquella. She, on the other hand, is asked to avoid mentioning in her improvisation the name of the slave's father, since that would render the following scenes redundant and spoil the dramatic effect (Andrews 2008: 11, 18). Such stage directions, addressed directly to the actors rather than describing what the characters do, are exceedingly rare and may in fact be considered an anomaly, because in a well-developed scenario form, no other instructions are normally necessary. From this perspective, Scala's warnings may be considered a compositional concession to his reading public. His intended readers were not professional actors and were therefore not accustomed to reading a scenario in order to visualize a performance text in the making. For the professional actor playing the slave, the technical notation for self-concealment known as an *osservatoria* – a simple asterisk, Perrucci (2008 [1699]: 193) informs us – would have been sufficient. Ideally, through a dialectical interplay of enablements and restraints, the scenario form gave the actor both the freedom to improvise the performance text and the narrative logic by which that freedom must be contained at every point of the plot. The improvisation of a given scene must lead to the beginning of the following scene in the scenario.

Read from the actors' perspective, a scenario is a tool for the visualization of the performance text using the author's guidance and the raw material already in their possession, actually stored in their memories and ready to be filtered through their imaginations. In this sense, the scenario prompts the actors to engage in a creative process analogous to that which Aristotle recommends to playwrights. In the *Poetics* Aristotle observes that, before composing the text of a play, the playwright should visualize its performance and then transport it into language (1455a22). Working with a scenario, commedia dell'arte actors transported visualizations into the performance text they are engaged in composing by improvisation. The scenario gave the actors the creative freedom to articulate the content of a scene, but at the same time it protected the plot from any excessive latitude they might be tempted to grant themselves at any point of the action. It worked as a grid for selective memory, prompting the actors to retrieve from their consciousness the most appropriate raw material in their possession, but it thereby also worked to protect the plot from the disorder that might ensue if the performer were not given the restraints of scene succession. The beginning of the next scene outlined in the scenario works teleologically on the creative consciousness of the actors like a final cause pulling their improvisation to the point that it must reach for the scene to be both thematically complete and artistically exact.

Improvisation

To understand this process, it may be helpful to consider a scenario in terms of its sources and its possible expansion into a scripted play. Among early scenarios, Giambattista della

Porta's *La trappolaria* holds a special place because we know with certainty its source text, Plautus' *Pseudolus,* and because the author expanded his scenario into a fully scripted play, also called *La trappolaria* (1596). In the transcodification of Plautus, Della Porta changed the names of the characters, added a few secondary characters of his own and provided explicit insertion points for *lazzi,* specifying the thematic content of those that are incorporated into the plot. The players of the *Trappolaria* scenario, first made available in print by Andrea Perrucci in his treatise on acting (Perrucci 2008 [1699]: 187–92), could thus study the *Pseudolus,* commit its content to memory, and recycle it in the improvisatory process, using their own words and gestures. When Della Porta transformed the scenario into a full sript, he changed again the names of the characters, eliminated the *lazzi* and *lazzi*-like episodes, and transformed the rest of the content into a lively dialogue. In this example we can catch a glimpse of the imbrication of the improvisatory process with the tradition of literary drama, a glimpse clear enough for us to reject at the start the romantic notion that stage improvisation might be an *ex nihilo* sort of creation. On the contrary, the *Trappolaria* allows us to argue by induction that all improvisation can be largely regarded as a matter of recycling previously scripted material, re-elaborating it to suit a plot and characters with a different appearance, and thereby transplanting it into the artisanal and aesthetic domain of the contemporary entertainment industry, wherein it becomes an improvised performance text.

Though new in Renaissance theatre, the concept of improvisation as a form of recycling old material had enjoyed uninterrupted currency in rhetoric since ancient times. For an orator speaking off the cuff, improvisation was largely a matter of creatively rehandling previously acquired material relevant to his theme. The same thing was true of an improvisatory player: speeches, quips and pithy lines acquired from literary sources constituted his repertory pieces which enabled him to improvise his character's behaviour in a particular scene. If he had a sufficiently large repertory at his disposal, a repertory with many analogous and equally suitable pieces for a dramatic situation, he could, moreover, change the performance script from one day to the next. He could also, of course, make use of the same repertory piece in a similar dramatic situation in other scenarios, altering it where necessary and always in his own words.

The economic advantages of improvised performances made such a specialization highly desirable and explains why so many contemporary actors turned to it. From an artistic point of view, the idea of a brilliant stage performance must have had the same appeal as that of music virtuosos, who were rising to fame at the same time in another area of the market. The virtuosity of an improvisatory player is based on the strength of his memory and the assiduousness of his literary studies. The most celebrated historical sources on commedia dell'arte leave no doubt on the matter. The actors Pier Maria Cecchini (1628: 19), Nicolò Barbieri (1634: 27–8), and Évariste Gherardi (1741 [1st edn 1700]: 5r; 1970: 58), and the scholar Andrea Perrucci (2008 [1699]: 196) all stress the importance of a strong and cultivated memory, filled with material ready to be used when the occasion might arise on stage in any play whatsoever – to be used, that is, creatively, refashioned into a new performance text directly on stage. It is this creative refashioning of memorized material that we call stage improvisation. We admire this creativity particularly in scenes depicting a character who needs to get out of a fix, as Harlequin frequently has to do in Goldoni's *Servant of Two Masters*. In such scenes the character and the actor both improvise their way to success – the one with his cleverness, the other with his acting skill – and 'seem to share in the pleasure of the play' (Crohn Schmitt 2020: 7), enhancing in the process the aesthetic experience of the audience.

Gherardi discussed in exceedingly clear terms the mechanism of text production entailed by improvisatory playing, as he and his Italian companions practised it in the Comédie Italienne company at the theatre of the Hôtel de Bourgogne in Paris. He placed the accent on the creative part of the recycling process, stressing that an actor equipped with the appropriate body of knowledge (*un homme qui a du fond*) can use his imagination to think in character, thinking his responses as he delivers them, within the constraints of the scenario and of the physical and verbal vocabulary of the actors on stage with him, in order to utter something to which they can respond in their collaborative composition of the performance text – that is, to their creation of composite units of text – under the eyes of the audience. Their collaboration is a form of stimulus and response chain in which their words and gestures must be so perfectly joined as to induce the audience to think that the text was previously composed and rehearsed (*à faire croire à tout le monde qu'ils étoient deja concertés*: 5v). In composing dialogue and physical interaction by means of composite semiotic units of performance text, the actors are guided by the probability of eliciting an appropriate response to which they can themselves respond. When this stimulus-response mechanism in the face of uncertainty is analysed in modern semiotic terms, it can be shown that the actors' intuitive grasp of response probabilities plays a crucial role in the logic of the improvisatory process and in the form of the performance text thus produced (Pietropaolo 2016: 69–73).

In this context, the word *form* has an aesthetic as well as a structural valence. Aesthetically, it refers to the source of the audience's satisfaction in their reception of the play and the provenance of their sense of its artistic beauty. Gherardi says that *la plus grande beauté* of an improvised play as a work of art is due entirely to the actors, who confer on the dramatic action of the scenario the right aesthetic qualities (*agrémens*) as their creation of the text is in progress (*jouant*). Gherardi's observation on the artistic beauty of an improvised performance has a remarkably modern flavour. In the language of the aesthetics of formativity, it may be restated as the principle that the source of aesthetic pleasure in the reception of an unscripted performance text is a *forma formans,* an artistic form in the process of becoming, achieving the state of a *forma formata* or a fully developed form only in the mind at the end of the reception process (Pareyson 2009: 165; Pietropaolo 2022: 511). At that point the audience should be unable to tell, says Gherardi (1741 [1st edn 1700]: 5v), whether what they admired was the form of a scripted or an unscripted play.

Lazzi

Among the sources of a play's artistic beauty, what Gherardi calls its *agrémens*, the *lazzi* of the most skilled actors are without doubt the most conspicuous. Scenario writers, fully aware of the showstopper potential of *lazzi,* provided convenient places for them or explicitly called for a particular type of *lazzo* in certain scenes. For example, in the scenario *Il convitato di pietra* or *The Stone Guest* (Oreglia 1968: 43–55), the commedia dell'arte antecedent of Mozart's *Don Giovanni*, there is an explicit and frequent call for *lazzi*. The second half of the first act is replete with requests for *lazzi,* mostly in the plural, indicating that more than one *lazzo* might be inserted at that point. The nature of the *lazzi* to be performed is specified only twice – in a scene requiring both a *lazzo* of the lunatic and a *lazzo* of day and night – at an insertion point where the author wanted the theme of the act to be integrated into the plot.

Integrated *lazzi* would be expected to contribute to the plot's sense of continuity: their removal would noticeably weaken its logical development at that particular point. On the plane of the performance text, their function is to articulate details of the dramatic action as a function of the expected behaviour of characters. All other *lazzi* are, by comparison, free-standing performance units without any special connection to the plot. The plot, however, is not the dramatic action of the play, but its organization into a narrative composition. The fact that a *lazzo* is not integrated in the plot does not necessarily imply that it has no relevance to the dramatic action (Fitzpatrick 1989: 186). The *lazzo* may not be meant to reinforce the plot's sense of continuity, but the play's aesthetic value would definitely suffer from its loss if it were not performed at that point. Its performance may be said to represent a planned momentary slowing down of the plot's movement, while the actor engages in a piece of bravura business designed to enliven the scene and elicit laughter. Such *lazzi* are portable performance pieces, and their main task is both to signify the brilliance of the performer and to inject ebullience into the scene.

On the plane of the play's thematic content, single *lazzi* may have complex implications for our understanding of the play as a whole. An effective way of sorting out those implications is to consider the semiotic relationship between a *lazzo*, understood as a small signifying unit, and the thematically relevant aspect of the dramatic action, understood as a complex semiotic entity with a message for the audience. Their relationship may be analysed in terms of the idea of semiotic opposition, developed by Juri Lotman (Moro 1993: 68). The most common semiotic oppositions in commedia dell'arte are those between servant and master, foolishness and cleverness, lust and love, and other dialectical articulations of social tension. The audience's recognition of the dialectic at work in the play may significantly affect their interpretation as well as their appreciation. Thus, *lazzi* collected by modern editors (Capozza 2006; Gordon 1983) under the rubric of comic violence can signify for the audience that the abuse of *zanni* by their masters is built into the structure of society, while *lazzi* of erotic mimicry among the servants may signify that the sentimental love of their masters is an artificial construct, though *lazzi* of animal mimicry may signify that *zanni* are animal-like to begin with and may be so treated without reproach. A semiotic perspective on *lazzi* has the advantage of showing the relevance of individual bits of comic business to the message carried by the main action. The analysis does not undermine the artistic unity of the play as a whole and reminds the audience that sometimes a very serious thought is at work in a roar of laughter.

The provocation of such laughter and reflection is an intended function of the performance text rather than the scenario, and it is to the players' performance text that the audience reacts. While they are not the authors of the dramatic action, the players are the authors of the performance text that gives that action the aesthetic materiality perceived by the audience. Their creativity is contained by the boundaries of the scenario, which gives them constraints for the semantic content of their utterances and provides them with appropriate places for the performance of *lazzi*. Working within these constraints, the players improvise dialogue by collaboratively forming binary units of vocal and gestural speech, each in the form of a stimulus-response combination, as they react to, and provide each other with, cues until the end of the scene. They perform visually and vocally, though not always verbally, all in accordance with the *concertatore*'s dramaturgical plan for the desired impact of the play.

Disciplined awkwardness

A major difference between Northern and Southern commedia dell'arte concerns acting style and performance conventions. We can appreciate the difference by citing two contemporary sources, one from the North and the other from the South. The first source is Pier Maria Cecchini, a celebrated first *zanni* with the name of Frittellino, who observed that Neapolitan actors could not be easily imitated by Northern ones. He noted that, on Northern stages, Southern characters were generally performed without the special grace of speech and gesture that they required and that only Southern players could give them, and so they frequently appeared as embodiments of vulgarity of speech and turpitude of movement. Neapolitan actors, on the other hand, could represent their characters with artistic grace and technical refinement. Cecchini cites in particular two famous contemporary Southern actors whom he had the pleasure of seeing on stage: Girolamo Buonhomo, in the role of Coviello, and Bartolomeo Zito, in the role of a Neapolitan version of the Dottore. Both performed their roles 'con quel verisimile che forse non ha simile in tutta Italia' (Cecchini 1628: 33), that is to say with a sense of verisimilitude hard to imagine anywhere else in the peninsula. Such refinement should not be misconstrued as an innate ability of Neapolitan actors; on the contrary, it should be recognized as the fruit of appropriate training and much reading.

The second source is the Southern scholar and playwright Andrea Perrucci, who explained that, whereas Northern troupes were excellent at representing complex plots, the Neapolitans excelled in *lazzi* and other routines of physical acting, and he cites the dictum, according to which spectators interested in good plot material should look to Northern commedia, while those interested in difficult *lazzi* should definitely look to the South: 'Neapolitan *lazzi* and Lombard plots' (Perrucci 2008 [1699]: 181). He cites nocturnal scenes played in the light by means of gestures and movement without dialogue. Southern actors typically performed the darkness that surrounded their characters by doing such things as moving gropingly into their playing area, bumping inadvertently into each other, and hesitantly climbing stairs without the assistance of a lantern. In addition to giving their gestures an expressive function, by which they could communicate the state of mind of the character, Neapolitan actors were accustomed to giving the same gestures a referential function, by which they indicated the darkness of night using the physical language of their bodies rather than speech. The darkness in the fiction of the story became a semiotic function of their acting techniques. By contrast, Perrucci observes disapprovingly, in such scenes Northern actors would not play the darkness but would instead use the occasion to give a performance of slapstick beatings. Their purpose was to raise the audience's laughter with the buffoonery of comic violence, whereas their Neapolitan counterparts were focused on generating in the audience the impression of darkness by a studied use of gestures of awkwardness and uncertainty.

Such gestural business was termed *disciplinata goffaggine* or controlled clumsiness by Cecchini (1628: 34), who used the expression in particular with respect to Pulcinella. *Disciplinata goffaggine* is a felicitous expression with a precise technical valence, and it is applicable to the character and the performer at the same time. *Goffaggine* refers to the character, who appears to suffer from a coordination disorder of some sort and hence lacks all grace of movement. *Disciplinata* refers instead to the actor performing the character's clumsiness with skill and art, exercising great control over something that appears to be uncontrolled. The audience laughs at the character's awkwardness while admiring the performer's art. By focusing on this trait in his examination of Southern-style commedia dell'arte, Cecchini calls our attention to the fact that actors of the Neapolitan entertainment market, unlike Northern actors, were rightly famous for the sophisticated use of their bodies in their impersonation of characters. And he speaks of them with great admiration: the performance of studied awkwardness, he says, is what dispels melancholy from the soul of the audience.

4

Commedia dell'arte and Ottonelli's theology

There is a conceptual analogy between the incorporation of actors into a repertory company, wherein their claim to expertise is warranted by a body of players of recognized excellence, and the incorporation of their performances into the semiotic fabric of society, wherein their claim to aesthetic value and truthful representation is warranted by the appreciation of the audience and the actual existence of the social conduct that the performers imitate. Incorporation, says Jacques Rancière in his political analysis of aesthetics (2006: 57), is a state in which incorporated elements can be regarded as a valid expression of the incorporating body, which they epitomize, aesthetically and ideologically. The incorporation of the theatre into the culture of the major institutions of society authenticates its claim to being a valid instrument of aesthetic gratification for the individual and an analogical tool of self-analysis for society. Disincorporation would instead be the result of a rupture between the theatre and the institutions around it, a sign that they are working at cross purposes and in a state of tension with official culture.

The main purpose of this chapter is to examine some of the issues involved in the incorporation of the commedia dell'arte of the seventeenth century into mainstream culture from the perspective of Catholic theology, which, in the wake of the Counter Reformation, was one of the great shaping forces of history. Its concern with the theatre, as with any other social activity, was focused on the ethical ideas regulating every aspect of life, particularly the relationship between individuals and their surrounding social institutions, and moved from the premise that a legitimate theatre could be considered integral to the body of a culture if it exercised a positive influence on the self-reflection and social conduct of individual spectators. The theatre creates fictions, on stage for direct observation and aesthetic enjoyment, and in the mind for lingering contemplation after the show, and fictions have a very real effect on the life of society because they challenge individuals to consider for themselves a different possibility of being.

As critical categories, incorporation and disincorporation enable us to study the state of theatre in society from a perspective that is at once ideological and aesthetic. In the commedia dell'arte of the sixteenth and seventeenth centuries, company directors were agents of incorporation, in both senses of the term: they incorporated actors into the company by recruiting them on the basis of talent, and they sought to incorporate the company's performances into mainstream culture on the basis of their aesthetic yield and ideological suitability. Since there was no market for individual performers working on their own, actors had to join a company in order to survive (Ferrone 1985: vol. 1, 12), sharing its collective sense of purpose. It was the task of the company director to clarify that purpose and to make sure that the company was as ready as possible to cater to the public of various cities. To gain status in mainstream culture was for the company to enter a lucrative area of the entertainment market, always with the hope that this might lead to higher and better forms of sponsorship, such as the patronage of dukes and princes, whose permission the company needed to perform in their cities. Without such cultural legitimation, a company risked remaining disincorporated in the margin of society, aesthetically as well as ideologically.

Disincorporation is a natural state for any theatrical group that operates on the fringe. The comic shows of mountebanks and charlatans in the marketplace were conspicuous examples of a disincorporated theatre. Such comic shows continued to survive alongside, and in frequent osmosis with, comedies by professional commedia dell'arte players. In a precious self-reflexive scene of his scenario *La fortuna di Flavio* (*Flavio's Fortune*, 1611) Scala offers us a clear view of the extent to which piazza performances penetrated professional commedia. Led by Harlequin, a troupe of charlatans are shown in the act of setting up a makeshift stage in the piazza and putting on a sales-pitch performance (*imbonimento*) of product demonstration, song and dance that quickly turns into a hilarious knockabout melee (Scala 1976: I, 34). There is no question, however, that professional actors, who performed with the constraints of a well-structured scenario even in their most farcical shows, felt they were entitled to a more dignified status in the dominant culture. For Andrea Perrucci, for example, charlatans gesticulated like madmen and sputtered obscenities, mangling whatever plots they tried to perform by improvisation (Perrucci 2008 [1699]: 102). The Neapolitan actor Gennaro Sacchi complained in *La commedia smascherata* (*Comedy Unmasked*, 1699) that the aesthetics and ideas of the great unwashed were still making it difficult for urbane commedia dell'arte to achieve integration into the cultural life of polite society (1.15). The plebeian aesthetics of histrionic buffoons, performing on stage in a theatre or on a bench in the marketplace, was not always separated from the urbane aesthetics of legitimate actors, although there were frequent calls for its separation. Consequently, there was much confusion among the arbiters of taste and morals, because it was difficult to discern a precise line of demarcation between the two types of performance and the categories of performers they involved.

The Church and society

The most important arbiter of taste and morals was the Church. Since its earliest history, the Church had presented itself as the mystical body of Christ composed by the incorporation of individual Christians into a single entity, a collective body in which each authentic member was an exemplary expression of the whole. Baptism was its sacrament of incorporation because it brought individuals into the body of Christ. On occasion the Church disincorporated from itself those who had strayed away, following, as Dante would say, false images of good (*Purg.* 30.131). Showmen intent on generating laughter figured prominently in that group. Until St Thomas Aquinas came round, with his rational approach to things human and divine, mainstream theology had nothing but fire and brimstone for laughter-inducing forms of entertainment. Such authoritative sources as the *Glossa Ordinaria*, for example, condemned everyday laughter as gravely sinful and deserving of severe retribution (Jones 2019: 22). But St Thomas, with his usual equanimity, taught in his *Summa Theologica* (II.IIae.q168) that a humorous thing could provide much needed rest for the soul. We should not only allow ourselves to enjoy such a *ridiculum* when it is produced for our entertainment, but we should also provide it for others to enjoy. To be sure, the excessive pursuit of fun for its own sake is detrimental to human reason and hence to the soul, and hence it is sinful. But by the same token, so is the denial of fun, because the soul must have repose from the toil of existence no less than the body. Aquinas' approach to the production and reception of *ridicula*, and by extension comedy, could be incorporated into the activities sanctioned by the Church. The golden rule was to exercise moderation in the pursuit of fun or laughter.

Soon after the Council of Trent, Aquinas was declared a Doctor of the Church, and his *Summa Theologica* became the standard textbook of theology in Italian universities. His authority was unchallenged and was regarded as unchallengeable. In this climate it is no wonder that the main work on commedia dell'arte from the perspective of the Church is called *Della Christiana Moderatione del Theatro* (1648–52), by the Jesuit theologian Giovanni Domenico Ottonelli. This is a long and complex theological and philosophical critique of contemporary theatre practices, examined in five weighty books (issued in six volumes in the 1656 edition), all focused on establishing precise parameters for legitimate stage entertainment. In the title of this work, the key word is *moderatione*, understood as the criterion of a possible consensus on the legitimization of comedic practices for a Christian community. The title page itself explains the author's perspective, specifying in the subtitle that the author's analysis of comedy is in accordance with the teaching of St Thomas, *secondo la dottrina di S. Tommaso*, and other theologians.

Ottonelli's *Della Christiana Moderatione del Theatro* is a farraginous work, with conclusions and arguments reappearing in different guises in various volumes, but it is by far the most substantial of the treatises on comedy issued by Thomistic scholars in the wake of the Counter Reformation, including very brief works, like the compilation of passages in defence of contemporary comedy by M.R.P., an unidentified theologian known only by these initials who collaborated with the Andreini players (1604), and a highly polemical tract, partly in response to M.R.P., by Domenico Gori (*c.* 1604) arguing against comedies and actors that promoted indecency, as well as a more ponderous treatment by Girolamo Bartolomei later in the century (1658). For all these authors, moderation means what scholastic theology and the Aristotelian philosophical tradition called the virtue of *eutrapelia*, the distinctive quality of all forms of recreation and entertainment that do not seek to produce an excess of pleasure and hence that do not cross the boundaries of rationality. As Gori says, eutrapelia is the virtue that informs all the comedies that the audience should seek to see, avoiding all others (Gori 1604: 143). Ottonelli discusses eutrapelia in much greater detail, under its own name (1648: 9, 49) and, throughout his work, under the name of 'moderation'. In the process he cites Aquinas and the major Thomistic philosophers of the Renaissance and Counter Reformation who can help elucidate the implications of the concept for contemporary comedies, scripted as well as unscripted. He also frequently refers to the works of eminent representatives of the commedia dell'arte itself, including the actors Francesco Andreini, Pier Maria Cecchini and Nicolò Barbieri along with others of lesser note, though his knowledge of actual performances is largely based on eyewitness accounts by others (1648: 49).

Ottonelli casts his critique in the form of an appeal for intervention by his ecclesiastical superiors and, especially, the civil authorities. Ottonelli argues that, for plays to be acceptable to a Christian community, professional troupes must curb their tendency to go to excess, both in what they represent and in how they represent it. He believes that the purpose of the state is to ensure that people enjoy freedom, peace and good mental health, and he contends that actors who are not guided by a criterion of moderation, especially improvisatory players and, among them, women performers, undermine this purpose by indirectly promoting vices, presenting bad judgement in a good light, and enhancing the appeal of immoral acts (1649: 182 and *passim*). Hence, he argues, moderation must be imposed on actors and playwrights by civil authorities, including aristocratic sponsors, on the advice of the Church, which already teaches such moderation through its preachers, bishops and theologians.

More specifically, with respect to the content of comedies, Ottonelli's position is that comedies are perfectly acceptable if they are performed by virtuous and honest players, and if their content does not subvert the values of a Christian community. But in his judgement, contemporary professional players, with their obscenities, can sabotage the foundations of society, even if all they intend to do is make the audience laugh. His main preoccupation in this regard is that many plays revolve around love affairs with married and unmarried women. Such plots promote adultery and disregard the sanctity of matrimony, the sacramental nature of which the Catholic

Church had only recently had to defend (in the 24th session of the Council of Trent) against formidable opposition from Protestant Reformers. The fictional adulteries of comedies also encouraged disrespect for civil authority, which counted on the stability of marriage to warrant the security of the social order (Ottonelli 1648: 205).The fact that, in comedic plots, the appeal of romance coupled with a promise of marriage caused fictional young women to enter into secret relationships with men might embolden real young women in the audience to yield to similar promises with potentially disastrous consequences. The fictional stories of contemporary plays indirectly taught married women how to commit adultery with impunity, and provided men with examples of successful love affairs and even abductions. With respect to the manner of presentation, Ottonelli complains, repeatedly, that the plot material is articulated by means of lascivious gestures and vulgar language, with ostentatious coarseness both verbal and physical.

Ottonelli singles out the *zanni* and maidservants, who do all they can to facilitate their masters in their nefarious pursuits, as the worst offenders, indeed as creatures of devilish nature (1652: 60). When the *zanni* and maidservants meet, he observes, they touch each other, make indecent gestures and use coarse language, giving rise to salacious and turbulent fantasies in the audience (1652: 297). Worst of all, however, is the fact that they perform by improvisation, because this means that there cannot be any external control of what they say and do on stage. Cultural incorporation into the community is next to impossible, unless, of course, the community resorts to coercion, imposing a standard of moderation through a board of censors. This was standard practice in the post-Trentine period, as the actor Nicolò Barbieri indicates by citing the authoritative example of Cardinal Carlo Borromeo, who agreed to allow commedia dell'arte performances in Milan, subject to his prior approval of the scenarios (Riverso 2016: 37; Taviani and Schino 1982: 209–10). Ottonelli would like the players to act always *ex scripto*, as he says, because that is the only preventive measure that the authorities can actually impose (1652: 299). If there is no script, he says, let them write out their parts and submit them for review; if the practice is to read a play and then to improvise the dialogue on stage, let them be properly advised as to acceptable stage behaviour and let them take an oath that on stage they will not cross the boundaries of decency. If they persist in crossing those boundaries, Ottonelli states unceremoniously, 'siano castigati' (1652: 296), let them be disciplined. If ideological incorporation proves impossible on a voluntary basis then let the authorities intervene with the necessary means of coercion to make it possible by obedience.

Women on stage

In the seventeenth century, the commedia dell'arte introduced into its dramatic form the expectation that its stories were located on the boundary between the private and public life of women (Tylus 1997: 327). Women could lean out from an upper-level bedroom window in the set to converse amorously with men below, in imitation of Venetian courtesans who appeared at their windows to entice prospective customers with suggestive glances. The way female characters moved and spoke on the set invited fantasies about what the actresses themselves did or could do in their private space, which was invisible to the eye but open to the imagination.

The melding of characters, actresses and courtesans in the sensuous perception of performance was not lost on Ottonelli, for whom, unlike ordinary women, actresses were skilled at using their eyes and faces to awaken erotic urges in the men looking at them – not only as fictional women conversing with the equally fictional men in the play, but as actresses addressing themselves to the real male spectators in the audience. Moreover, they had at their disposal an entire repertory of phrases and speeches with which to strengthen the erotic power of their glances (1649: 170–1). It was natural, therefore, for a theologian to ask why so many women, who could earn a living doing something else, embraced this profession, in which they dressed to titillate the imagination and spoke pruriently of love, 'lascivamente ornate e parlanti d'amore' ('lascivously adorned and speaking of love'; 1652: 13), at the service of a dramaturgy that made use of their bodies to market erotic entertainment as aesthetic experience.

In answering this question, Ottonelli shows that he was not unaware of the plight of the working poor, among whom women suffered greater privation, 'con i quotidiani sudori e stenti' ('with daily sweat and hardships'; 1648: 115). Here Ottonelli spoke eloquently and with unusual sensitivity of women trapped by their birth in a distaff economy, in which they could hope for nothing better than a life of social repression and long hours of work for meagre earnings. For such women – and it was from their class, Ottonelli believed, that many performers came – the stage, even that of a very modest venue, was a promise of liberation, the possible fulfilment of their natural ambition to overcome restraints and to be honoured for their talent. Such fulfilment was a concrete claim to aesthetic and ideological freedom. On the aesthetic front, it represented freedom to express feelings and ideas in a public performance for compensation, while on the ideological front it constituted liberation from the stronghold of the moral majority. Ottonelli sympathized with the predicament of working-class women but he felt compelled by his theological convictions to argue against their choice of the stage over normality in society. A huge obstacle to the theological acceptance of women on the comic stage was the familiar misogynistic attitude that regarded femaleness as the portal through which the devil caused the fall of mankind. Eve, Ottonelli reminds his readers, was also moved by an appetite for greater honour (1648: 115), an appetite that afflicts all women like an inherited disease.

It is entirely possible, of course, that decent and well-intentioned women, respectable in every way, might want to earn a living as players. But for Ottonelli their good intentions were not enough to justify their presence on stage, since even innocent actresses could set a spectator's imagination on fire and cause him to lose the light of reason (1648: 141). The fundamental problem for Ottonelli was that the beauty of an actress could throw the intellect of men into disorder and lead them to court their own spiritual ruin. Ottonelli did not take explicitly into account the distinction between actresses who achieved success by cultivating the capacity of their minds as well as the beauty of their bodies, actresses like Isabella Andreini, who lived in accordance with the highest moral standards of society and the Church. Indirectly revealing much about his own sexual anxieties and fixations, Ottonelli focuses his criticism on the sensual appeal of women players, particularly those who, lacking education and opportunities to cultivate their minds, had little else to lend to the profession other than their bodies and their talent in using it to communicate ideas and sentiments. But it is the display of female beauty as such, even when it is not superlative, that Ottonelli finds gravely dangerous to men, whether the intention behind the display is libidinous or chaste, and whether the actress is refined or not. All actresses on stage appear beautiful, even if they are not so in reality. After watching a play, a husband may easily find his wife 'molto piú brutta, piú vecchia e piú disgraziata' (much uglier, older and more ungraceful, Ottonelli 1648: 141). The author here invites the reader to draw the inference that the physical beauty and other charms of an actress may be responsible for a male spectator's marriage problems and the disharmony that they may give rise to in the family. This is because actresses who are not naturally pretty adorn themselves to fool the eyes of a spectator and skilfully use the sweetness of their voices and the studied gracefulness of their movements to enhance the erotic appeal of their bodies (1648: 143), to the grave danger of the men in the audience gazing at them with fascination.

Ottonelli's concern is much greater when the troupe includes an actress who intentionally transgresses the boundaries of decency in performance. He is concerned for the weaker souls in the audience, 'anime poco stabili nella vuirtú' (1648: 160), especially when the performers add dance to their words. In order to dance, actresses wore male costumes that enabled them to move like *zanni*. It is likely that Ottonelli, who spent many years in Sicily, had in mind a *zanni* costume like Coviello's, sufficiently suggestive of musculature and shapeliness to evoke salacious fantasies. For Ottonelli a woman's appearance in men's clothing was not only unseemly but bordered on monstrous hybridity (1648: 164). Even so, if an actress dressed up as man, and if her only purpose were to cause honest cheerfulness, that is eutrapelia, by dancing decently before a group of morally strong (*forti di spirito*) people, she would not commit a sin. The problem was that, in a public theatre, most spectators who sought such entertainment were in his view spiritually weak to begin with and could easily lapse into lascivious thoughts upon seeing such an actress on stage. Ottonelli knew of many young men who sinned repeatedly in their imagination ogling a cross-dressed pretty actress flexing, contorting and twisting her little body, her *corpicciuolo*, in a dance (1648: 168).

It is noteworthy here that, instead of calling the actress's body her *corpo*, using the standard form of the word, Ottonelli preferred to call it *corpicciuolo*, a caressing term with suffixes that enrich the neutral description with attributes of slimness, delicateness and gracefulness, simultaneously conveying an unmistakable sense of endearment on the observer's part. *Corpicciuolo* is a word that implies prolonged contemplation of the dancing female body, either in reality or in thought. Experiencing as he probably did the power of his own libidinous imagination, even as he subdued it to the dictates of theological reason, Ottonelli had some understanding of the men in the audience who were all too prone to yield to the visual pleasure of the dance. Yet in the aesthetic of the pantomimic body, *corpicciuolo* describes the adolescent frailty of the performer's body together with a sense of participatory sympathy on the part of the observer, suggesting that, in his perception of her movement, the performer appears to be subjecting her body to a strain that it cannot endure for long. And so, *malgré lui*,

Ottonelli's style also reveals his commiseration for the young woman who, having freed herself from a life at the distaff or the spindle, now earns a living by laboriously forcing her small body into unnatural and erotically charged contortions, under the illusion that this activity brings her the honour of art rather than the dishonour of erotic vulgarity.

The lesson implicit in Ottonelli's analysis is that a theological reading of the commedia dell'arte is first of all an aesthetic reading, focused on the sensuous perception of the show and the experience of pleasure that it evokes in the imagination. The aesthetic perspective, however, becomes quickly ideological as we realize that morally weak spectators may be overwhelmed by their sensuous and imaginative experience quite simply because they are not mindful enough of the ethical restraints within which they must remain to preserve their innocence before God and to help safeguard their families and society from disorder. Commedia dell'arte troupes, Ottonelli argues, should contribute to this containment of the male psychology by restricting the appearance of women on stage. He would gladly sanction the incorporation of commedia troupes into the fabric of culture, but only on the condition that they impose heavy restraints on their female players. The principle at work here is the familiar patriarchal idea that, being temptresses whether they want to or not, women are responsible for the sexual fantasies of men and carry the burden of protecting the community from the disharmony that such fantasies may generate.

The appearance of women on the commedia dell'arte stage, performing with impunity activities at once beautiful to watch and to fantasize about, represented an assertion that men should bear full responsibility for their own psychology and for any unethical behaviour to which their fantasies may lead them. At the same time, it was a blow to the patriarchal limitation of the freedom women had over their bodies and their individuality as members of society. A theological treatment of commedia dell'arte could not possibly avoid the challenge that it thus issued to the fundamental premises of the social theory of the Church. Ottonelli accepted the challenge and made a valiant effort to expose the implications of performing women for the moral health of the audience and the stability of the institutional order of society.

PART TWO

Innovations in the eighteenth century

PART TWO

Innovations in
the eighteenth
century

5

From scenario to script:

Riccoboni and Goldoni

In so far as dramatic form is concerned, mainstream commedia dell'arte of the seventeenth and eighteenth centuries may be conveniently visualized as a continuum from scenario to script. Between these polarities, there are partly scripted scenarios in which the playwright and the performers were called to collaborate on the authorship of the text embodied in performance. Advocates of the scripted form objected to scenarios because they gave performers an authorial function for which they lacked the ethical and literary qualifications. Ignorant or unscrupulous players could use a scenario to generate immoral content and illiterate language. Ottonelli, as we have seen, objected to the open form of a scenario chiefly on moral and theological grounds, and he launched his attack from outside the theatre world. But in the eighteenth century serious objections to the scenario form were also voiced by professionals in the theatre itself, indeed by professionals who had a leading role to play in the history of the commercial stage, chief among them Luigi Riccoboni and Carlo Goldoni.

Luigi Riccoboni

Riccoboni set forth most of his criticism of scenario-based theatre practice after his eleven years of experience in Paris as director of the Italian Company, the Comédie Italienne, at the theatre of Hôtel de Borgogne (1716–27). The Comédie Italienne, which had been disestablished in 1697 by Louis XIV, was renewed in 1716 by Phillip II Duc d'Orléans, who recruited Riccoboni from the resident company of Teatro San Luca in Venice and offered him the helm of the Italian theatre in Paris. In addition to being an accomplished actor and company director, Riccoboni was also a playwright and theatre scholar of no mean repute, but he achieved distinction especially in the role now known as a dramaturg and which commedia dell'arte companies then knew as *concertatore* (Ferrone 2014: 209; Perrucci 2008: 193; Pietropaolo 2006: 93–4). In Italy Riccoboni belonged to a circle of scholars and playwrights concerned with the reform of Italian literature, still heavily entangled in baroque aesthetics on account of which it was under vigorous attack from French scholars. Many rose to its defence, Riccoboni among them. In this circle, Riccoboni had quickly espoused the concept of *buon gusto* (good taste), understood as a faculty of aesthetic discernment, a cultivated ability to distinguish between art and non-art. He applied the concept to the commercial theatre which, dominated as it then was by low-level commedia dell'arte, seemed in urgent need of reform.

Riccoboni thought that virtually the entire repertoire of Italian scripted plays needed serious dramaturgical revision. The best plays of the *commedia erudita,* for example, needed heavy editorial cuts in order to become stageworthy and some rewriting to pass as morally acceptable works of literature (Riccoboni 1973: 25). In this proposed dramaturgical doctoring of the plays in the canon, he went as far as to suggest replacing some of the characters with new ones. But his major concern was with outlining principles of dramatic form suitable for a new-play development dramaturgy in the context of mainstream commedia dell'arte. He distinguished between plays in verse and plays in prose, which, beyond a shared five-act structure, had a decidedly different artistic form. In the composition of new poetical drama, he recommended replacing masked characters with more appropriate unmasked ones, since the association of commedia dell'arte masks with ludicrous laughter seemed aesthetically incongruent with the literary elegance of verse. For the same reason, he proposed that poetical comedies be written and performed in pure Tuscan, without a trace of the dialects conventionally spoken by the masked characters.

New prose comedies, however, could retain both the masked characters and their dialects in the performance text, since actors skilled in masked performance could add a special mark of artistic excellence to a play, to the great distinction of both Italian comedy and performance practice. Such distinction, however, could not be achieved if the dramatic action itself was ludicrous, ungoverned by rules of structure and oblivious to the requirements of *buon gusto*. In the eighteenth century, these aspects of dramatic theory were discussed under the rubric of the rules of artistic unity, that is the unities of action, place and time derived from the Renaissance interpretation of Aristotle's *Poetics*. This pseudo-Aristotelian concept, accepted as a dogma of dramatic structure in the Renaissance and beyond by Italian literary comedy, by the beginning of the eighteenth century was on the forefront of the discussion concerning the reform of all drama, including commedia dell'arte. The rules do not concern the wording improvised by actors in performance – though the criterion of *buon gusto* certainly applies to them – but the author's conception of the dramatic action and the form into which it was organized as a plot. Any call for reform in that connection was directed at the scenario writer and not the actors.

Riccoboni's position in regard to the scenario is that it should be possible to perceive the action as if it were real.

This is the aesthetic criterion of verisimilitude, on which all other aspects of form, including its sense of unity, ultimately depended. In the prologue to the scenario *Il filosofo deluso*, Riccoboni explains that he violated the strict interpretation of the unities of place and time, but that this was fine because the action had a clear true-to-life quality, that is it was conceived in accordance with the principle of verisimilitude (Riccoboni 1973: 105). For Riccoboni, the story must always be told in such a way as to be believable. To respect this principle it may be necessary to interpret the rule of unity of place generously so as to allow the playwright to shift the location of the action by a reasonable distance. For the same reason, Riccoboni advocated understanding the unity of time as an interval long enough to allow the inclusion of episodes a little beyond the one day of the conventional interpretation.

In his consideration of the formal aspects of unscripted plays, Riccoboni's concerns can all be reduced to this: as a dramatic form, the scenario of the received tradition was too permissive a structure in that it granted the actors a greater creative role than was appropriate. However moral was the intent of the author, and however precisely he had built the dramatic outline of his scenario, unscrupulous actors could always find room for the insertion of verbal and gestural text that was morally and aesthetically reprehensible. For even a scenario that observes the rules of thematic decorum may be used to produce a scandalous comedy on stage (Riccoboni 1738: 218). Unlike a scripted play, in which the author exercises a high degree of control over the actors' output in performance, a scenario is a permissive framework by nature, and this may cause even excellent actors to diverge. 'La liberté qu'ils ont de dire ce qui leur vient à la bouche, peut séduire quelquefois les comédiens les plus circonspects' (Riccoboni 1738: 219). In this statement Riccoboni makes clear that his criticism is directed at nothing other than the creative freedom that is inherent in the concept of improvisation itself. The words *ce qui leur vient à la bouche* are in fact an exact translation of a classical Latin definition of improvisation (Pietropaolo 2016: 55) *quid quid in buccam venit*.

Riccoboni on the reformed scenario

If it is considered from the perspective of someone determined to control the creative process in view of its intended outcome, such freedom is not at all the positive thing that it may appear to be to actors. The temptation to give themselves a larger authorial role than is implicit in the built-in intentionality of the scenario may prove to be too great for even the most accomplished actors. Good actors are *circonspects,* always careful to avoid going in any direction that might take them away from the framework of the scenario's intentionality, but even they occasionally yield to the temptation of freedom.

The solution proposed by Riccoboni is that the dramatic form itself must be altered to prevent licentiousness from taking place. The framework must be reconceived in such a way as to make its intentionality explicit in exclusionary as well as inclusionary ways. The scenario must not only convey to the actors what they should do and say in the performance text but must also constrain the actors from doing or saying anything that might take them beyond the moral and artistic parameters intended by the playwright. In so far as they are regarded as performance errors, exclusions cannot be explicitly listed in the scenario. The scenario, however, may make it very difficult for an actor to go astray. In composing his own scenarios, Riccoboni says that he was governed by the need to include constraints of this type, as he remarks in a note in his *Discorso della commedia all'improvviso*: let his critics examine his scenarios carefully, he observes, and they will see just how much he endeavoured not to leave room for any maliciousness in the improvisatory process (Riccoboni 1973: 31). The result is a new type of scenario in which the description under the rubric of each scene are so detailed as to be a rendering in indirect speech of the dialogue and attendant activity to be produced by improvisation. In virtually every scene of his *la moglie gelosa* (*The Jealous Wife*) and *L'ubriaco* (*The Drunkard*), for example, Riccoboni summarizes the details of the intended performance text so scrupulously as not to leave any room for the insertion of unwanted remarks or gestures without disrupting the flow of text from one character to the other.

Riccoboni is aware that scenarios of this type may be too prolix and hence too demanding for typical players. In general, scenarios were traditionally very concise, their scene descriptions being no more than a few skeletal indications that required little or no preparation. Riccoboni's proposed scenarios required much study and an approach to acting that was still generally unfamiliar to Italian actors: 'un'arte poco nota sin ora a' comici italiani' (Riccoboni 1973: 32). Italian actors working in the commedia dell'arte tradition were not accustomed to the idea that such restrictions could be imposed on them from within the scenario. In Riccoboni's reform of unscripted comedy, they were required to study the scenario very attentively and commit it perfectly to memory so that they could perform it by improvisation without leaving out or changing any of the details given in the summary. Moreover, the actors had to play their parts without making it awkward for their stage partners to pick up the flow of the dialogue in their collaborative creation of the performance text. For Riccoboni, the achievement of a perfect artistic reciprocity between the actors, understood as a readiness to be mutually beneficial to each other's creative role, is a necessary condition of smooth textual flow in improvisatory performance (Cappelletti 1986: 94; Riccoboni 1728: 62).

As a dramatic form, Riccoboni's reformed scenario is somewhere between a traditional scenario and a scripted play. It differs from a conventional scenario because it imposes performance reciprocity and reduces the possibility of undesirable improvisations, and it differs from a scripted work because the final wording of the text is still to be produced. But it is clear that production of the final text in performance by improvisation is conceived by him as the final stage of the author's writing process, carried out orally through the agency of actors working under his vigilance. Riccoboni's reformed scenario comes very close to becoming a scripted play, though it does not cross the boundary.

Goldoni's transition to script

Goldoni's best known contribution to the commedia dell'arte is *Il servitore di due padroni* (*The Servant of Two Masters*), which he wrote for the troupe of Antonio Sacchi in 1745 as a scenario, with only a few speeches for the serious roles and a skeletal outline of dialogue and actions for the comic roles. The version that everyone knows, however, is not the original scenario but the fully scripted one completed by Goldoni in 1753, when he had already worked out and put into practice all the details of his famous reform programme. In his letter to the reader of this edition (1996: 97), Goldoni openly declares that *Il servitore di due padroni* had already made a very successful debut as a partly scripted play, with a performance text brilliantly improvised by Sacchi's troupe. In his scripted version, he made every effort to retain some of that brilliance, writing lines that could give the audience the impression of performance spontaneity without, in fact, giving the actor much creative freedom. Even in the moment of fleeting self-reflexivity in which Truffaldino, in an aside to the audience, says (in Venetian) that he is trying to get out of trouble by improvising lies as best he can, *digo quel che me vien alla bocca* (177), the actor is, of course, reciting scripted words, through which Goldoni recalls for spectators in the know the Latin definition of improvisation, *quidquid in buccam venit*, only to show that no improvisation is actually taking place, whatever may seem to come spontaneously to Truffaldino's lips.

Antonio Sacchi, who was a highly skilled improviser, may have said exactly these words when he first played the role of Truffaldino by improvisation, prior to Goldoni's scripting of the play, and Goldoni may well have transcribed Sacchi's performance. But in the printed edition of the play familiar to modern readers, the intended performance text of this delightful layering of identities, in which Sacchi pretends to be Truffaldino who, through Goldoni's transcription, imitates an improvisatory player like Sacchi in the act of citing a famous definition of improvisation, is entirely under the control of the author. With the hindsight of historians, we can see that the model of scripted textuality towards which the hybrid scenario reached out was the one envisaged by Goldoni in his reform programme. In the paragraphs that follow, we shall turn our attention to that part of Goldoni's programme that concerns the concept of dramatic form.

The key to Goldoni's views on the dramatic form of commedia dell'arte plays and on the modifications to which it can be subjected is *Il teatro comico* (*The Comic Theatre*), a play about a company in the act of rehearsing another play, *Il padre rivale del figlio* (*A Father His Son's Rival*), starring the traditional commedia dell'arte characters. At the end of the 1749 season, when he was on contract as resident playwright with the company of Girolamo Medebach at the Sant'Angelo theatre in Venice, Goldoni promised the audience sixteen new comedies for the following season. *Il teatro comico* was one of the new plays, the one that Goldoni later regarded as an introduction to all the others and possibly to his entire oeuvre, so well did it express his idea of a theatrical reform. In the course of the rehearsal, the process of writing and performing comedies becomes a major question of discussion. *Il teatro comico* is thus a dramatized poetics of comedy in which Goldoni outlines, in the manner of manifesto commitments, the points on which he intended to hinge his reform programme for the commercial theatre of Venice.

First among these is a distinction between plays in the repertoire of the commedia dell'arte tradition and plays in the reformed style, which Goldoni calls *commedie di carattere*, or character comedies. Placida, the fictional prima donna of the company rehearsing the play, refers to conventional *commedie dell'arte* as boring, claiming that the audience virtually always knows what the likes of Harlequin are likely to say even before they begin to speak (Goldoni 1983: 38). The words *commedie dell'arte* in Placida's statement are the first recorded occurrence of the famous phrase. The expression is used in the plural form, to indicate plays performed in the manner of the professional companies, as suggested by the word *arte*. The phrase, however, soon became popular in the singular form and was treated like the denomination of a homogeneous genre or style, by scholars, playwrights and actors of later generations, and eventually applied retroactively to the entire tradition, from the Renaissance to the present. Whether or not Placida was right in her assessment of the commedia dell'arte of her day, Medebach and Goldoni were experiencing considerable success with the latter's *commedie di carattere*. A second actor in the fictional rehearsal, Tonino, who played the role of Pantalone, complained in Venetian that such plays were disrupting the acting profession: 'Le commedie de carattere le ha buttà sottosora el nostro mistier' (Goldoni 1983: 39). An actor trained to perform by improvisation in the commedia dell'arte style was now required to study a script, commit to memory the words of the author, and learn to produce them as if they were his own. Goldoni intimates that many actors found it difficult to adapt.

Goldoni's usual composition process prior to his reform was as follows: he first conceived of a dramatic action, then he created its characters, wrote the dialogue and finally matched the parts to the actors and cast the play. Since some actors found their parts unsuitable, Goldoni reversed the second and fourth step in the process. First, he devised the action; second, he examined the personality and peculiarities of the members of the company, secretly casting the play; third, he created characters matching the personalities of the actors and then wrote the dialogue accordingly. Only at that point did he officially cast the play. The reform implication of such system was that he could train actors to make the transition from unscripted to scripted plays with little difficulty.

Goldoni on character comedies

The professional environment of the commedia dell'arte conditioned actors to be somewhat hostile to the performance style of scripted plays. The transition to character comedies implied a radical adjustment of the skill set required of professional actors. As an actor, Medebach was obviously willing to make such an adjustment, and as a company director he was willing to impose it on his players. But not everyone was of that mind, and even within individual companies there was some discontent, since the actors were given little latitude for creativity. Character comedies were fully scripted and had to be performed exactly as they were written and not paraphrased in the actors' own words. The author exercised control from within the text itself. Goldoni's persona in the *Teatro comico*, the company director Orazio, explains that the actor's vocal and gestural dynamics, the varying loudness of his voice, as well as the tonality and rhythm of his utterances and the expressive use of his hands must be in strict accordance with the meaning intended by the words in the text (Goldoni 1983: 80). Whereas a scenario required the players in the cast to assume a significant authorial role in generating the performance text, and whereas a scripted play performed in the commedia dell'arte manner allowed the players the creativity of paraphrasing the text, the script of character comedies was meant to exercise full control over them, who were required to serve it to the best of their abilities by performing it without interjecting anything of their own invention. If Riccoboni wanted to control improvisatory acting to ensure respect for the intentionality of the scenario, Goldoni aimed to get rid of the scenario altogether, proposing to change the performer-centred commedia dell'arte concept of a play into one based on a script-centred and playwright-driven dramatic form.

If it was to have literary as well as dramatic merit, such a form must be sustained by an internal principle of artistic unity, which for Goldoni meant no more than that the play should observe the classical unities of action and time. The form was the logical shape of a single, concisely conceived action that unfolded without digressions. The value of the third classical unity, the unity of place, seemed debatable. In the strictest interpretation possible, the unity of place was understood as unity of scene, and hence as a requirement that the action take place in the same theatrical set. Goldoni regarded this rule as so illogical that, as far as he was concerned, Aristotle himself would readily argue against it if he were to return to life in the eighteenth century. Only the simplest plays could be produced with this rule; most plays would end up being a combination of absurdities, if changing the set were not an option. In his reform of the commedia dell'arte, Goldoni proposed interpreting the rule of the unity of place liberally enough to allow set changes if the action took place in nearby locations, say in different rooms of the same building or in different areas of the same city. Like Riccoboni, he believed that the only essential rule was that of verisimilitude, which should never be sacrificed for the sake of so foolish a rule as the one prescribing unity of place (Goldoni 1983: 58).

Plays written in the reformed style retained the three-act structure and, at least for a while, even the masked characters of conventional scenarios. Through Orazio, Goldoni explains that a reform must be carried out gradually. While the actors must learn to act in the new style, the audience was asked to relinquish its loyalty to inherited conventions. The masked characters could not be suddenly removed from all plays because the audience paid good money expecting to see them. From the success of his early character comedies, Goldoni surmised that, unlike the Venetian audiences of old, the spectators of his day also appreciated serious parts, refined language, clever action developments, a story with a useful moral and witticisms, all of which would have been rare in traditional commedia dell'arte. Venetian spectators were not ready, however, to give up the masked characters altogether (Goldoni 1983: 67). Until they were ready, he thought that the masked characters should continue to appear in scripted drama, though behaving in a morally acceptable manner. At this stage of his reform, Goldoni therefore retained the masked characters but in writing out their speeches, he purified their behaviour of all vulgarity, adding social decorum to their conduct and a touch of literary grace to the text flowing from their lips.

6

Riccoboni's commedia of civic responsibility

Luigi Riccoboni's programme of reform is rooted in his study of dramatic literature, a field in which, already at a young age, he had acquired familiarity with what we might call the canon of classical and post-classical drama (Mamczarz 1973: xxx). As director of the Comédie Italienne, he had planned to produce a number of Renaissance literary comedies, expurgated of obscenities, enriched with examples of moral virtues and invested with a didactic purpose. But Riccoboni ran into difficulties when he was still in his first season (1716–17). The audience did not respond well to the literary aspirations of his programme and could not appreciate the literary merits of the plays. The Italian language was not as well known as Riccoboni had hoped, and the Parisians were nostalgic for commedia dell'arte (Trott 2000: 55). Attendance was poor, and when he was persuaded that the theatre had lost enough money, Riccoboni reverted to commedia dell'arte, with its scenarios for improvisation and stock figures, including its traditional masked characters, still much loved by the theatre public.

There was no reason, however, why he could not attempt to change the course of Italian theatre, or at least of the comic Italian theatre produced in Paris, from within the commedia dell'arte itself. The scenario form and the stock characters were just as susceptible to dramaturgical creativity as their counterparts in scripted comedy. We have already seen the changes that Riccoboni's reform dramaturgy brought to the elements of form, adjusting the scenario, character attributes and performance techniques of traditional commedia dell'arte in such a way as to prevent any slippage into lasciviousness. In this chapter we will examine how, with his adjusted form, Riccoboni sought to contribute to public discourse, using comedy as a collective podium for civic engagement. We shall examine Riccoboni's systematic effort to bring a sense of civic responsibility into the commedia dell'arte by injecting into the scenario a conspicuous sense of social ethics.

For Riccoboni comedy must have a clear didactic function and a strong moral purpose. In his prologue to *La moglie gelosa* (*The Jealous Wife*, Riccoboni 1976: 40), he says explicitly that comedy should aspire to become a good school of morality and an effective tool for the correction of behaviour, but also an aesthetically pleasing form of laughter-generating entertainment for the public theatre, whose function it is to please those who are innocent of the ways of the world as well as those who are well acquainted with its unsavoury manners. To this end he proposed a model of comedy designed to use humour as an instrument of good citizenship, all in the context of an aesthetic of verisimilitude, in which a work's artistic merit is a gauge of its perceived truthfulness and relevance.

As an aesthetic principle, verisimilitude presupposes the existence of an external reality whose aspects can be placed in a one-to-one correspondence with the formal elements of drama and hence combined into a play. The form of the play may thus be regarded as an assemblage of signifiers, while its content may be seen as the set of signified people, actions and places that constitute aspects of reality. The aesthetic of verisimilitude judges the artistic merit of the work by its verifiable truth-to-reality character and by the appropriateness of the signifier–signified combination. Verisimilitude requires characters with some psychological depth, their emotions resembling a little those of the audience, who should be able to identify with them as people encountered in their own experience.

The compositional process begins with the aspects of reality that can generate such experiences and proceeds to link them to the signifiers (characters, words and actions) that can represent them without appreciable distortion. By the late seventeenth century, when the masked characters had lost much of their relevance to the social reality from which they emerged, commedia dell'arte seemed to follow the reverse process, starting with a set of signifiers linked to each other by inherited functional relationships and injecting aspects of reality into them, so as to construct an artificial world on stage rather than to describe the real one off stage. The significant question concealed in the aesthetics of verisimilitude concerns the aspects of social reality selected for representation. In the rest of this chapter, we shall look at two examples of Riccoboni's selection, one dealing with the ethics of marriage, *Il filosofo deluso,* which illustrates the virtues that can help society, and the other, *L'ubriaco,* which illustrates the vices that can destroy it.

Ethics of marriage

Il filosofo deluso (The Disappointed Philosopher) is a play in the commedia dell'arte tradition, complete with masked characters and all manner of *lazzi.* Though they are traditional laughter-inducing devices bordering on the ludicrous, the *lazzi* are neither obscene nor scatological. They have a farcical character and involve physical as well as verbal language, but the quips and foolish speeches that punctuate the more serious side of the action are never morally coarse. Thus, for example, the scene in which the Philosopher splutters a tirade against his wife (I.v), the one in which Flaminia's tears the academic robes off her husband and gives him a punch or two (III.v), and the scene in which she gives Harlequin (Arlichino in the text) a good beating (III.vii) are all typical of the commedia dell'arte style, but they do not require the sort of vulgar stage behaviour with which improvised comedy had been saturated in recent years. The masked characters do not have major roles, and a couple of them are cast in a non-traditional way: Scaramuccia is a servant and the Dottore a secretary.

The dramatic action at the centre of the play is a love story leading to marriage, as in many other commedia dell'arte plays. Here, however, there is no hint of lasciviousness and no detail of language, gesture or theme that might generate images of licentiousness in the audience. Silvia and Mario, two students of philosophy, who are entirely guileless and untouched by any form of vulgarity, fall in love and secretly pronounce marriage vows to each other. The taking of such vows in secret constituted what was known as a clandestine marriage, valid even in the eyes of the Church until the Council of Trent ruled against it, but no doubt still practised in the age of Riccoboni as a secular form of marriage to be later sanctioned by parental consent. We are not told how old the two students are, but it is likely that they are only teenagers, since in France at that time most people married in their late teens, long before they reached the age of majority – twenty-five for women, thirty for men (Roulston 2010: 9) – and hence required parental consent to marry legitimately in the eyes of the community. The scenario presents Silvia and Mario as innocent and without any experience of the less honourable ways of the world – a detail by which Riccoboni sought to dismiss from the audience's mind any suspicion that the couple's love might be tainted by lasciviousness and hence that they might be considered undeserving of sympathy. Moved by the depth of their feelings, they decide to marry each other secretly, going against the explicit teaching of Silvia's father, who is also their philosophy professor. By the end of the play, however, the Philosopher becomes persuaded that mutual love is the fundamental principle of a healthy marriage and gives his seal of approval.

Il filosofo deluso is set in Paris, and the location is significant, because the play was meant chiefly for the Parisian audience of the Comédie Italienne. Both before its closure (1697) and after its reopening under Riccoboni's direction (1716), the Comédie Italienne operated in a culture deeply concerned with the concept of marriage. In all social circles, it seems, the institution of marriage was at the centre of a debate fuelled by the ongoing conflict between the Church and the State concerning who had regulatory authority over it. The emotional nature of the bond of married or betrothed couples, which had previously been a matter for private contemplation, had entered the arena of public debate and socially engaged fiction, where it was linked to policies and rules for the proper organization of society. In this climate, observed Joan DeJean, writing about love and marriage 'was hardly an innocent gesture' (DeJean 1991: 11). DeJean was referring specifically to the growing number of women writers of fiction, but her statement is also valid for authors of dramatic scenarios, whose work was meant to be performed in public theatres, wherein it could provide entertainment but also influence public opinion. With *Il filosofo deluso,* Riccoboni wished to enter the debate, using the stage as a didactic platform and humour as an instrument of argumentation.

Il filosofo deluso is a clear example of the type of civic engagement that Riccoboni wanted to build into comedy. In his treatment of marriage, Riccoboni reveals two important aspects of his approach to reform. The first is that he conceived the comic theatre as belonging to that genre of writing that is conventionally called advice literature, that is literature giving practical counsel on matters of social and family life. Since it deals with ordinary people in everyday situations, comedy can easily assume the function of advice literature if it is conceived from a perspective of ethical responsibility. In this sense, the teaching function of the theatre must be based on the principle that the stage should be incorporated (in Rancière's sense of the term) into the life of society, not only as a place of diversion but also as an agent of the official culture, advising prospective

marriage partners on the proper way of getting married. The
second aspect of Riccoboni's reform programme is the fact
that the theatre must contribute to the betterment of society. It
must, that is, be a vehicle for social reform as well.

In order to be consistent with an aesthetic of verisimilitude
and play a part in the rectification of undesirable trends,
dramatic representations of love and marriage could not
include any of the sexual games of traditional commedia
dell'arte plots, even if similar acts were actually found in
society. That comedy should represent selected aspects of
society in a credible manner does not imply that it should
reproduce them on stage as exact copies. In the case of love
and marriage, comedy should create a fiction representing
the ideal to which actual marriages should reach out in their
pursuit of fulfilment. In the early eighteenth century, the idea
itself of marriage was being slowly reconfigured, as parents,
in arranging or approving a union, began to take into account
the will and mutual attraction of the prospective bride and
groom. Silvia's and Mario's marriage is a dramatic narrative
of that shift in focus, in which the sentiments of the couple
have come to the foreground. That does not mean, however,
that sentimental love has displaced parental consent and
social convenience. It means rather that love has joined
parental agreement as an equally necessary criterion for the
legitimation of marriage.

This is accomplished in a highly original way. In a delightful
scene, Silvia, dressed as a young man, tells Mario's father,
the Marchese, that she is a good friend of his son. With her
attractive manner and courteous words, she so impresses him
that he wants the two young people to promise solemnly to
remain good friends for life. Mimicking a marriage ceremony
in both gesture and language, the Marchese joins their hands
and asks them to promise in his presence to love each other
until they die. The irony of the situation is that he does not
know that the friend is a woman and that the two of them
had already married in secret. By performing this friendship-
bonding ritual in imitation of a wedding ceremony, which is

focused on the same sentiment, he in effect sanctions their clandestine marriage. The only other thing necessary for their marriage to be regarded as legitimate is consent from the father of the bride and disclosure of the secret, both of which happily come at the end of the play. By giving his approval, the Philosopher acknowledges the centrality of love in a proper marriage, thereby enabling the couple's clandestine celebration to emerge publicly as a reflection of the community's ideal for the organization of society.

Moral corruption

In the prologue to *L'ubriaco* (*The Drunkard*), Riccoboni says he is confident that he has appropriately sketched out the consequences of Pantalone's excessive drinking. The punishment reserved for him in the plot, articulated as a catastrophe that he brings upon himself and his family as well as his business, at first appears to be extremely serious, but in reality is very much attenuated by an unexpected turn of events in the plot. The consequences of his becoming oblivious of his duties as a father and as a member of his community do not actually take place: Pantalone's daughter does not ruin his family's honour by running away with a lover, his servant Harlequin returns the money that he stole from his master, and his son is wounded but not killed in the duel he fights to defend his father's reputation. If Riccoboni had not decided to mitigate his castigation of the drunkard, he would have had to allow his daughter to run away with impunity, and while by doing this the author might have delivered Pantalone the blow that he deserved, in the process he would have shown young women in similar circumstances how to get away by following their own bad judgement. If he had conceived a dramatic action centred on punishing Pantalone, the author would have committed the error of unwittingly teaching daughters another vice, that is, how to determine their own fate without parental consent. Riccoboni avoids the error by making Pantalone believe that his life has fallen apart – that is to say, by inflicting only psychological punishment on him – until the end of the play, when he learns that his son, supposedly killed in a duel, is alive and well and ready to ask for forgiveness. Riccoboni's purpose here was to cause the audience to leave the theatre with the conviction that the drunkard was sufficiently punished, that the requirement of parental consent was protected and that mutual consent should be accepted as a necessary foundation of the institution of marriage.

There is no denying that all of society is afflicted by alcohol abuse, but it is interesting that, in his dramatization of the pervasiveness of this vice, Riccoboni should focus on a social milieu between the common citizen and the aristocrat. By the beginning of the eighteenth century, the traditional criticism of drunkenness as a sign of moral dissolution was given a new twist. Drunkenness among the rich continued to be regarded as a vice of debauchery leading to personal ruin, whereas among the working poor it began to be considered as a form of misconduct leading to disorder or crime in the community (Rabin 2005: 457). In short, the new discourse on alcohol consumption had a political character at the lower social end and a personal character at the upper end, implying social consequences of a different gravity between these extremes.

It is against the background of this discourse, particularly in the articulation that it was given in Paris, where alcohol consumption was notoriously high, that Riccoboni's scenario was meant to be performed by improvisatory players. In this comedy of civic engagement, the author and his players sought to contribute to the advancement of that discourse in contemporary culture, assuming a position of moderate chastisement with respect to its main issues. In the prologue to *L'ubriaco*, Riccoboni says that a comedy should not offend the morals and sense of decency of polite society, 'della civile società' (Riccoboni 1973: 57). Such offence might be generated by an unrestrained condemnation of drinkers that does not take social class into account. A dramatic action of this kind would in any case place drinking and drinkers in the limelight, and hence in the consciousness of the spectator, at the expense of its remedy. The purpose of comedy is not to overindulge in the representation of a vice under the pretext of correcting it, calling more attention to the vice itself than to its correction, but to portray it in such a way as to shift the aesthetic interest of the audience from the vice of excessive drinking to its consequences on the family and the community. Riccoboni was confident, however, that in his scenario he had managed to castigate the vice of drunkenness without offending anybody in particular and in a way that would cause both the common man, *cittadino*, and the nobleman, *signore*, to fear the sort of catastrophe that could befall them if they habitually indulged in alcohol abuse (59).

The drunkard chosen by Riccoboni to illustrate the dangers of alcohol abuse is not an aristocratic *signore* but Pantalone, characterized as a well-to-do business man, fully engaged in the economy of his community. He overindulges habitually and at times is dishevelled and unable to fulfil the obligations of his profession. He forgets important business meetings, is easily duped into signing false documents (72), pays little or no attention to the welfare of his family, with the consequence that his daughter is tempted to run away with a lover to the dishonour of his family (75), and causes his servant Arlichino to rob him of his savings and his son to get wounded by Scaramuccia in a duel fought to defend his father's honour. Pantalone's drunkenness, in other words, is not characterized as the vice of a nobleman bringing about his personal ruin by overindulgence, but as the vice of a citizen who brings crime to his community and grief to his family. At the end of the play, when he finds out that his daughter is now safe and that his son's wound is not very serious, Pantalone acknowledges that the vice of drinking can lead to disrespect for social norms and the breakdown of the family: 'la corutela de' costumi e la rovina delle famiglie' ('the corruption of customs and the ruin of families', 80).

Pantalone's recognition of the error of his ways and its repercussions on the community lie at the focal point of the comedy of civic engagement advocated by Riccoboni. The scene has nothing in common with the farcical antics of old commedia dell'arte. The aesthetic experience of laughter-inducing performance, including such things as unsteady movement, forgetfulness and social foolishness caused by inebriation, is subtilized by the simultaneous expression of feeling. The result is a complex kind of humour that Riccoboni called *le comique du sentiment,* a form of the comic that he much admired in Moliere (Riccoboni 1736: 88). The intended cognitive experience of the audience is a pleasant feeling of human solidarity resulting from the recognition that Pantalone has rediscovered the sense of personal responsibility that can render him worthy of the civic fellowship of the audience. The play contributes to the public discussion of a shared concern and attempts to encourage members of the audience who have an inclination to excessive drinking to think about the consequences that their vice can bring to both the individual and the community. As a comedy of civic responsibility, *L'ubriaco* represents an effort to raise community awareness concerning the seriousness of alcohol abuse and to promote an attitude of moderation in its use. Comedy can thus entertain and participate in teaching good citizenship. For Riccoboni, the traditional stock characters, and the dramatic actions of which they were the agents, had little or no ethical content and hence no positive relevance to the life of the community on whose stage they appeared. With *L'ubriaco*, Riccoboni attempted to show how traditional commedia characters and stock themes could have a positive and constructive role when motivated by a sense of civic duty.

For Riccoboni the conceptual apparatus of commedia dell'arte need not be used merely to elicit easy laughter. He does not show a drunkard acting silly on stage, first because he thought that comedy was not exempt from the requirement of decorum by which civil society is governed, and second because the performance of laughter-inducing silliness together with the happy resolution of conflict inherent in comedy might actually lead people to think that drunkenness is not the unredeemable social evil that temperance-minded critics were ready to assert. By the beginning of the eighteenth century, the masked characters of the commedia dell'arte had virtually become empty signifiers, in the sense that they did not have immediately identifiable referents in contemporary society. For this reason, they could be shown engaged in ludicrous and irresponsible behaviour. The laughter and boisterous cheeriness that generally accompanied such forms of entertainment might promote the impression that the conduct of the characters was not as dangerous to society as some might claim. The analysis of a sample of commedia dell'arte scenarios by Luigi Riccoboni can give us a representative glimpse of the ideological dimensions of his reform of comedy. Riccoboni was motivated by a dramaturgy of social stewardship using conventional elements of the commedia dell'arte in a form that could redirect the audience's attention towards the ideal of a moral and stable community. His reform programme is informed by the idea that, in a dramaturgy of reform, commedia dell'arte can provide the audience healthy entertainment while imparting a lesson in good citizenship.

7

The commedia dell'arte in Goldoni's reform

In the introduction to the first volume of the 1750 edition of his comedies, Goldoni let his readers in on a secret. All that he knew and that proved useful to him in the practice of his art was the result of careful study of two metaphorical books: the World and the Theatre. He read them diligently, and there he found the logic of his poetics and the substance of his plays. He read real books as well, including all the books of normative poetics and the canon of western drama to his day, and he learned much from them, but that bookish knowledge did not serve him well in the practice of his art, the real sources of which remained for him the careful observation of life around him in society and painstaking attention to the conditions of production and performance in real theatres (Goldoni 1993: 628). The image of Goldoni's two-book source of dramaturgical inspiration is based on the principle that between art and society there can be a reciprocally beneficial symbiosis, an interaction that can be aesthetically advantageous to the development of art and ideologically advantageous to the development of society. In the paragraphs that follow, we shall examine these ideas in Goldoni's poetics of reform, chiefly as outlined in his prefaces and dramatized in *Il teatro comico* (1750), against the background of the commedia dell'arte prevalent in the commercial theatres of his day.

The World

From his study of the World, Goldoni derived the social dynamics of his plays as well as some character types and plot functions. Before he gathers material for his plays, the playwright must determine the aspects of society (beliefs, customs, passions, habits) that deserve support and promotion and those that deserve opposition and criticism. The playwright should pay special attention to, and eventually mine for his plays, social values and aspects of behaviour familiar to all, 'che son piú comuni del nostro secolo, e della nostra nazione', that is, the most common in our century and in our nation (Goldoni 1993: 629). By turning such observations into the primary stuff of his dramaturgy, the playwright can make his art socially relevant and contribute to the progressive incorporation of the stage into society.

The notion of relevance makes dramaturgical sense if the audience recognizes that what the playwright has to say on a certain topic is imbricated with their own self-understanding as citizens and with their grasp of the logic by which the life of their community appears to be governed. The attainment of such recognition, and any subsequent reflection to which it might lead the audience, is the anticipated result of a playwright seeking to be relevant. Goldoni makes this very clear in his preface to the first volume of his collected works, where he observes that the vices and deficiencies that afflict the country deserve to be castigated and ridiculed by the wise, 'meritano la disapprovazione e la derisione de' saggi' (629). This statement is tantamount to a poetics of comedy as social criticism, an assertion that the techniques of derision should be used to advance a particular view of society. In Goldoni's perception, social forces that work against the well-being of the community deserve to be degraded by humour. To achieve this goal, the characters and the action in which they are involved must themselves, in some way or other, resemble contemporary social reality, as incorporated elements that reflect the aspirations of the incorporating social body (Rancière 2006: 57). The stock characters of run-of-the-mill commedia dell'arte had become totally disincorporated from society. By the eighteenth century, for example, the patchwork of Harlequin's costume, which once represented the tattered clothes of the poor, had become a self-contained abstraction in the form of an aesthetically appealing multi-coloured geometrical pattern.

Against the abstract theatricality of commedia dell'arte, Goldoni envisaged fictional characters that came from the world of the audience, and he wanted them to appear in situations not unlike those encountered in real society. Goldoni was interested in representing aspects of society that deserved to be rejected by every thinking human being but also in depicting the traits of upright citizens, persons of unyielding integrity whose very existence benefited society. The book of the World, Goldoni says, always directs its readers towards the means by which virtue can safeguard itself from vice, 'i mezzi coi quali la virtù a codeste corruttele resiste' (629). Such means are exemplified by the actions of good people, who embody healthy social values. By creating fictional characters with their attributes, the playwright can contribute in an affirmative manner to the advancement of the discourse on social progress. It follows that the action of a comedy should give rise to a dialectical relationship between the negative and positive forces that shape the moral quality of the community to which the characters belong. Here 'dialectical' should not be understood, at least not primarily, as an element of form designed to motivate plot development. More importantly, it is a thematic tension intended to promote progressive social thought in the audience. For Goldoni, comedy is relevant not only because it can be a mirror of current social values but also because it can intervene constructively in their further development.

For Goldoni, the metaphorical book of the World contains aesthetic as well as social instruction. Socially, it points to the need for relevance and aesthetically it argues for verisimilitude, so that its ideological assertions may appear believable and its claims to artistic status may be persuasive. To achieve this credibility, he needed to observe reality very carefully in order to create plot situations and character types that, whatever specificity they may be given in a particular play, would be received as true to life because the spectators would be able to recognize themselves in them, and that is why they could enjoy the play. In his *Teatro comico*, Goldoni is unambiguously direct: when they recognize their own passions in those of the characters on stage, says Anselmo in Venetian, 'i omeni se sente a bisegar in tel cor' (men feel touched in their hearts, ii.1). Characters that are recognizable as authentic representations of real social types will always be liked (iii.9), but they must not be shown performing actions that undermine the true-to-life aspect of their conception. For example, Harlequin may not use a slapstick on his masters because in real life no servant would do such a thing. Nor should women be shown engaging in conversation with men in the street, because public decorum does not allow it to happen in reality.

The playwright should also avoid long soliloquies about the background of the story, because that is not something likely to be seen in real life. Indeed, even in writing a scenario for improvised comedy, the author should make it so that the players do not stray from verisimilitude ('per non distaccarci dal verisimile', ii.2). Whether scripted or improvised, a play should not include any details that might undermine the true-to-life effect generated by a well-conceived plot. Goldoni understood clearly that verisimilitude is predicated on the inclusion of plausible events and on the exclusion of language and behaviour that might appear inconsistent with the plausibility of the narrative in which the characters are involved. In the transitional period of Goldoni's reform, there are two kinds of verisimilitude: one in which masked characters, though not depictions of human beings, behave as if they were depictions of human beings, and the other in which the characters and their behaviour resemble human beings.

Goldoni's ideal of verisimilitude should not be misconstrued as an aesthetic of realism, that is to say an aesthetic of the literary and dramatic conventions for the mimetic representation of reality, with all the richness of detail and exact depiction that the term imitation ordinarily implies. Verisimilitude is not a synonym for realism. Though the path of realism leads to verisimilitude, it is by no means the only path with this aesthetic destination, nor is it always the most suitable one (Stoehr 1969: 271). In any case, realism could hardly be envisaged in a gradual transformation of the commedia dell'arte. On the other hand, an effect of verisimilitude can be achieved even in the representation of the stock characters. Given certain characters, masked or otherwise, lifelikeness is the impression created when they exhibit the same attitude to existence and society that the audience experience in their own life as social beings.

Goldoni's task is not the representation of unique individuals but the depiction of character types, because types make possible easy inferences about shared values. Character types are somewhat idealized – as are, for example, Pantalone in *Il servitore di due padroni* and Mirandolina in *La locandiera* – because Goldoni is not as interested in the exact representation of society as he is in promoting its improvement. As Anselmo says in *Teatro comico,* the social purpose of comedy is to correct vices and deride immoral behaviour (ii.1). In such a programme, idealized types are representative of large social groups in ways that unique individuals could not be. They are instruments through which the author seeks to intervene in the development of community values.

The Theatre

The areas of society on which Goldoni reflected most assiduously in the early years of his career were the social relations made available to his imagination by his daily experiences as a lawyer. From his training in law, Goldoni knew that the truth about complicated situations is frequently revealed little by little, and that fragments of truth have to be composed into a causal sequence by the imagination. Goldoni was very proud of his legal background, to the point that on the title page of every volume of his collected works he identified himself as a Venetian lawyer: 'Carlo Goldoni, Avvocato Veneto'. In the frontispiece of volume 9 (1761), he went as far as to present, with dubious taste, an interrogation under juridical torture. It may well be that the courtroom interrogation process furnished Goldoni with a model for the systematic discovery of a plot situation and for the progressive revelation of the truth behind an action. Certainly in his *Teatro comico* (iii.2), Goldoni observes that a gradual exposition of the facts is essential to the success of a play: 'the right way to present the situation without boring the audience is to divide it into several scenes, and little by little reveal it, to the pleasure and surprise of the listeners' (1969: 62). This observation takes us from Goldoni's reflections on the activities of the courtroom to his reflections on the theatre, where his focus is on audience response.

The pleasure and surprise of the audience are premises for the development of the performance-related strategies of Goldoni's reform programme. He sought, in the first place, techniques and tricks from the legacy of the commedia dell'arte, conventions that might help him present the masked characters in a way that would help the audience see that they had traces of real people in them, psychologically and emotionally if not physically. Until he decided that he should abandon the masked characters altogether, Goldoni continued to train himself as a playwright by studying contemporary performance conventions. In this endeavour, he did not neglect the lowliest form of the commedia dell'arte, namely the street shows of the mountebanks, with some of whom he had early established a friendly relationship. In Milan, for example, while temporarily on staff as a lawyer in the office of the Resident Ambassador of Venice, Goldoni came to know street performers of distinction in the Company of Buonafede Vitali. Better known to his contemporaries as the Anonymous, Vitali was once a learned professor of medicine and an author of scholarly works who had become a professional medical charlatan – professional in the sense that charlatanry was a form of medical practice licensed by the state office of public health (Gentilcore 2006: 2) – and the leader of a troupe of commedia players. His actors used street-performance techniques to peddle his snake-oil remedies in market places and to perform comedies in local theatres.

In Venice, moreover, Goldoni made a concerted effort to become acquainted with the techniques of the mountebanks who appeared with regularity in Piazza San Marco. In connection with his composition of the interlude *La Birba* (*The Rascal*, 1734), Goldoni recounts in his French *Memoires* that he studied with considerable care the verbal and physical language of street performers. He made use of their comical utterances and gestures and of their clever performance tricks, confident that, by incorporating them into the theatrical vocabulary of his interludes, he was actually sowing in the field of his creative imagination seeds that would one day ripen 'into an agreeable and profitable harvest' (1877: 185). Goldoni wrote these words as an old man, when he could consider the multivaried corpus of his large production in a single purview and see his youthful appropriation of marketplace commedia as a metaphorical seeding of his creative imagination. We may doubt, of course, that, as a young lawyer occasionally moonlighting as a playwright, Goldoni had the foresight implicit in the image of a fruitful seed. We can be certain, however, that, in writing the narrative of his concept of character comedies, the ageing playwright wanted his readers to know just how deep were the roots of his art in the commedia dell'arte, including its marketplace variety.

Goldoni, however, observed with greater care the personalities and mannerisms of the players in the company for which he worked as resident playwright. He focused on the real-life personalities and stage personas of all the players in the company, abstracting their peculiarities and applying them to the fictional characters that they were likely to impersonate. Goldoni understood that, for the script writer of a professional company, writing comedies that aspired to some degree of success meant writing within the constraints of the material conditions of the theatre. These conditions consisted mostly of the performers themselves, their native abilities and training as well as their personal inclinations. Trying to create characters that could not be easily impersonated by members of the company would have been tantamount to courting failure. On the other hand, to invent characters who, whatever their plot function, might appear tailor-made for the individual players, characters requiring precisely their skill set and their personal peculiarities, would be to create characters likely to be performed with success. In his *Memorie italiane*, the title under which modern scholars have gathered the prefaces to the Venetian edition of his plays issued between 1761 and 1778, Goldoni states that, in composing his plays, he always tried to adhere to this principle: that the characters should be designed to suit individual members of the company, whose typical mode of stage address, personal traits and professional abilities were already incorporated in the author's conception of the characters themselves (Goldoni 1983: 186). He illustrates this principle by referring to *La bancarotta* (*Bankruptcy*, 1741), a play he wrote for the company of Giuseppe Imer, which included members of uneven talent. Goldoni faced the challenge by writing for each of them a suitable part, like a coat cut to a perfect fit ('tagliata sul loro dosso') and requiring no more than their particular deportment ('e adattata alle loro forze') to be worn with elegance on stage (1983: 219).

A deservedly more famous example of Goldoni's technique from an early phase of his reform is the comedy *L'uomo prudente* (*The Prudent Man*, 1748), written for Cesare D'Arbes. This famous actor was a highly accomplished Pantalone to whom for some reason the audience had recently accorded a cool reception. Goldoni came to his rescue by writing a play in which the Venetian masked character appeared redesigned to allow D'Arbes to display his great skill as an actor. In this play, Pantalone is an upright merchant and an authoritarian father and husband. His much younger wife and his son (from an earlier marriage) attempt to poison him, but when their attempt fails they are arrested. Instead of seeking justified retribution, Pantalone becomes a wise, loving and generous man, and in the trial argues with passion in favour of their release, persuading the court that this is indeed the wisest course. In the process, Pantalone expresses powerful emotions which make him more human than traditional Pantalones and make him resemble a real father, recognizable as such despite his mask and costume. Goldoni's Pantalone has shed the unworthy moral baggage he had been dragging around on stage since the early days of the commedia dell'arte.

As a masked character, however, Pantalone could not use his face to manifest his emotions. Therefore, in impersonating his role, D'Arbes had to exercise much greater control of performance techniques than he would have had to do if Goldoni had followed the traditional way of characterizing Pantalone. The reason is that Goldoni's text required the actor to manifest emotions that were quite alien to the expressive vocabulary of traditional Pantalones. In the *Teatro comico* (i.4), Orazio, played by Medebach, recalls this success, and in *Memorie italiane* Goldoni reports that his new conception of Pantalone made *L'uomo prudente* hugely successful, while D'Arbes was acclaimed by all as a truly superior actor. In *Il padre rivale del figlio*, the play rehearsed by Orazio's troupe in the *Teatro comico*, Goldoni ennobles Pantalone considerably by putting him in a plot situation in which he acquires consciousness of his morally unacceptable behaviour and reforms himself of his own volition, as Jordan has shown (2014: 133),

The next stage in the reform of the Pantalone mask was the total humanization of his character. It was accomplished by Goldoni in two steps: first, by removing Pantalone's mask and costume, which liberated the actor from the movement and posture constraints associated with the character's traditional appearance, enabling him thus to make use of facial gestures in his expression of sentiments. Second, by giving the character the psychological features and physical mannerisms of the actor likely to play his role. This step would give Pantalone a personality that could be easily reproduced on stage by an actor making use of his own attributes and mannerisms as signifiers of the character's defining features. Goldoni followed an analogous procedure in his transformation of other commedia dell'arte stock figures into characters whose appearance behaviour, language and mode of being resembled real people of his time.

An example from the period in which Goldoni's reform programme was in full development is the character of Mirandolina, the innkeeper of *La locandiera* (*The Mistress of the Inn*, 1752). The role was the result of a transformation of the stock *servetta* of the commedia dell'arte into the successful owner of a small inn. Goldoni wrote the role of Mirandolina somewhat in haste for Maddalena Marliani, who, in Medebach's company, played the role of the maid Smeraldina. The 1752–3 season was about to open when Medebach announced to the company that his wife, the leading lady Teodora Medebach, had taken ill, and so they would have to mount a different production, since in the one with which they had planned to open the season, *Pamela*, a play based on Richardson's novel by the same title, Teodora had the leading role. Medebach asked Goldoni to put together a different script without a prima donna part, a script that the rest of the company could learn to perform in a short rehearsal period. Goldoni, who was suspicious of Teodora's frequent illnesses and who had feelings for Maddalena, seized the opportunity to transform the character of the maidservant into that of the inn mistress and called her Mirandolina. He endowed Mirandolina with a progressive vision of society, and gave her the attributes and mannerisms of Maddalena's stage persona. He was rightly confident not only that this would shorten the required rehearsal time but also that it would enable Maddalena to emerge as a star in the role of a champion of social progress. The play was so successful that, as Goldoni recounts, Teodora miraculously recovered and persuaded her husband to close the show and resume the season with *Pamela*.

At this stage of Goldoni's reform, the ontology of his *dramatis personae* is significant. In the performance text of a play, a character achieves material being as a hybrid of an abstract conception by the author and of the real person of the impersonating actor. But in Goldoni's poetics the hybridity already exists at the conceptual level of the author, who has already incorporated some aspects of the actor's personality into his construction of a character at the writing stage. Such an ontology is possible because, as we have seen, Goldoni reversed the relationship between composition and casting. Whereas ordinarily characters are invented and scripted before casting, Goldoni began by secretly casting the play and then proceeded to create the characters and write the dialogue. The success of Cesare D'Arbes in *L'uomo prudente* and Maddalena Marliani in *La locandiera* illustrates the principle that, for Goldoni, to write professionally for the stage means to write for a particular company, taking into account the strengths, weaknesses and peculiarities of its members. Only that way could the characters achieve verisimilitude in the performance text.

In later productions of plays, it would be the task of company directors to cast them correctly, matching character requirements with performer attributes, but in the first production the casting was always carried out by Goldoni before he wrote the play and before the characters were fully developed in his mind. The characters were in fact psychologically 'prefabricated' to suit the members of the company. So designed, the characters needed only to be assigned a role in the dramatic action and to be given lines to speak before the actors could give them life as plausible social types on stage.

8

Gozzi's fable form:

A new horizon of expectations

When Carlo Gozzi's *L'amore delle tre melarance* (*The Love of Three Oranges*) premiered at the Teatro San Samuele in Venice in 1761, commedia dell'arte had long been in a state of decline. Occasionally, audiences could still be treated to excellent improvised plays, but these could be regarded as no more than isolated flashes of brilliance in a tired tradition. The dominant reaction to the decline was to advocate for fully scripted drama, with plots increasingly grounded in the aesthetics of verisimilitude and with characters explicitly designed to be different from traditional commedia masks. Gozzi's reaction was to fashion a new dramatic form, with characters from commedia and plot material from fables of magic and wonder, articulated in a text that was partly scripted and partly improvised. In *The Love of Three Oranges*,

This chapter was first published, with minor differences, in *Three Loves for Three Oranges: Gozzi, Meyerhold, Prokofiev*, ed. Dassia N. Posner, Kevin Bartig and Maria De Simone. Bloomington: Indiana University Press, 2021.

Gozzi pursued his objective with a programmatic intent in collaboration with Antonio Sacchi's troupe of improvisatory players, expanding the creative domain of commedia dell'arte and providing Venetian audiences with a new horizon of expectations – formal and aesthetic – for the commercial theatre. In this chapter we shall examine the principles and techniques Gozzi used to create his new form and to determine the extent of the actors' contribution to its development.

In 1761, the principal members of Sacchi's troupe included Sacchi himself, an actor who had achieved great distinction in the role of Harlequin under the name of Truffaldino; his wife, Antonia Franchi Sacchi, who, in *Three Oranges*, was probably cast as Clarice; his sister Adriana Sacchi Zannoni, a talented Smeraldina; the renowned Cesare D'Arbes as Pantalone; Agostino Fiorilli as Tartaglia; and Atanasio Zannoni as Brighella (Taviani and Schino 1982: 112–14). Their widely recognized collective talent notwithstanding, Sacchi's company was going through a period of considerable difficulty, as was to be expected of actors who had remained anchored to the commedia dell'arte and were commonly regarded in the profession as champions of the dying art of comic improvisation. While Sacchi was trying to relaunch his troupe at the San Samuele, the companies of Girolamo Medebach at the San Giovanni Grisostomo and Giuseppe Lapy at the San Luca were riding the crest of success, having embraced new artistic mandates in collaboration with Pietro Chiari and Carlo Goldoni, respectively. Both playwrights sought to displace commedia completely from the commercial stage, replacing it with new, fully scripted plays in the different styles for which they were becoming increasingly famous – *commedie di carattere* in Goldoni's case and *commedie lacrimose*, or sentimental comedies, in Chiari's case. Gozzi agreed to provide Sacchi, gratis, with plays that would help Sacchi's company to re-enter competitively the theatre market by performing commedia dell'arte in a new key. This was not the first time that Gozzi collaborated with Sacchi, as recently explored sources in the Fondo Gozzi (Gozzi collection) of the Biblioteca Marciana have made clear; however, it was the first time that Gozzi saw Sacchi's troupe as the creative partners he needed to launch his new poetics for the commercial theatre (Vazzoler 2018: 18–20). *Three Oranges* was to be the first of a series of ten theatrical fables, and part of its task was to raise for the audience a new horizon of expectations in the commercial theatre. The players had a new and exciting artistic mission to work with and a greatly expanded horizon – for themselves and for their audiences – in which to display their talent. Gozzi would write for them plays melding fairy tales (*fiabe*), commedia dell'arte and criticism, both social and aesthetic – plays designed to re-establish the aesthetic dignity of stage improvisation and engage it in the ideological discourse of his class.

Gozzi's infantilist ethos

The production of *Three Oranges* could not have been more successful on that score. The original scenario did not survive, but from the account of the performance that Gozzi published more than ten years later, under the title *Analisi riflessiva della fiaba l'Amore delle tre melarance* (*A Reflective Analysis of the Theatrical Fairy Tale 'The Love of Three Oranges'*, 1772) we know that it was a resounding success (Gozzi 1962: 47–84). Its most appealing aspect was the frequent fusion of magic and humour: 'The Spectators had been informed by their nurses and grandmothers of all these marvels mixed with ridicule, and of the childish simplicity of these scenes since their earliest years. They were deeply immersed in the subject, and their souls were strongly captivated by the daring novelty of seeing such an accurate representation of it in the Theatre' (Gozzi 2021: 63). Magic had always been a prominent part of popular culture, but in the form and to the extent proposed in *Three Oranges*, it was entirely new. With this play, Gozzi was proposing the creation, on stage and among the audience, of an ethos of childhood, a pervasive sense of remembered fantasies and rediscovered pleasures of the imagination.

The incidents woven into the plot provoke recollections and engage the audience by generating in them a feeling of innocent suspense. This feeling is an experience of uncertainty concerning the outcome of a scene, coupled with the anticipated gratification that accompanies the ability to confirm, at least in part, the logic of its outcome by comparing individual incidents occurring on stage with images of analogous ones retrieved from the spectators' memory. The trick, Gozzi seems to suggest, is for actors to represent those incidents so vividly as to make the audience believe that their own recollections are being staged in the dramatic action. Endearing as it was, however, the ethos of this new artistic practice had at least two practical functions. The first was to expand the players' and playwright's control of the current entertainment culture; the second was to market, as aggressively as possible and in a commedia package, the audience's recollection of childhood fantasies and the gratification of nostalgia that normally accompanies them. In both functions, it was meant to generate a desire, a market, for plays set in a fantasy world. In this sense, Gozzi's plan does not appear to have been much different from marketing strategies familiar to us from recent history. 'The infantilist ethos', says Benjamin Barber with reference to the modern world, 'generates a set of habits, preferences, and attitudes that encourage and legitimate childishness' (2007: 81). The same principle is valid for the intersection between theatre and the economy in eighteenth-century Venice, with an important caveat: the destabilization of the divide between childhood and adulthood in the theatre was also part of a genuine interest in the renewal of drama as an aesthetic domain. On this front, the childhood ethos of *Three Oranges* was not tainted by the cynicism that informs many infantilist strategies of consumer capitalism.

We may hear a note of patronizing superiority in *puerilità*, the term with which Gozzi describes the simplicity of the incidents that so captivated the San Samuele audience. Still, the infantilism that Gozzi had in mind was a pretend return to childhood imaginings, much the same way that primitivism is a pretend return to a primitive way of life in the past, which in reality it purifies of its inconveniences and philosophically idealizes as a critique of the present. The *fiabe* that Gozzi wrote for Sacchi's players had the appearance of innocent childhood stories but were, in reality, laughter-eliciting allegories of the present, laden with uncharitable criticism of rival playwrights and theatre makers.

In Gozzi's estimation, it was precisely this combination of humour and imagined childlikeness that, in the first production of *Three Oranges*, elicited the most favourable audience response, consolidating his own quick ascendancy among the playwrights and Sacchi's among the actor-managers of the Venetian commercial theatre. When humour is recognizably directed at certain individuals or social groups, as it generally was in the commedia tradition, it is grounded in self-righteousness and tends to build solidarity, if not outright complicity, under an aesthetic cover of innocence. In an explicitly self-reflexive scene in Gozzi's *fiaba*, Zannoni, as Brighella, recommends commedia dell'arte as an innocent form of theatrical entertainment against melancholy-causing comedies in the style of Goldoni, represented by Leandro, or in the bombastic style of Chiari, championed by Clarice. As the actual effect of a perlocutionary speech-act, laughter is a means for both the playwright and the performers to castigate their rivals, drawing their audience into their own horizon of expectations.

The gambling culture and the theatre

In this horizon, concerns and ideas that inform the present can be dressed up as childhood fantasies and organized into a narrative of magical transformation and speaking objects. Childhood fables are used as a coding system for the theatrical representation of ideas that have nothing to do with fables. In *Three Oranges*, Gozzi is concerned with the theatrical poetics of Chiari and Goldoni, whom he satirizes with gusto in the vein of what he had started to do a decade earlier in his recently discovered play *Le gare teatrali (The Theatrical Competitions)*. But the ideas inspired by the Enlightenment, which the Venetian aristocracy had every interest in keeping outside the Republic, were also a target of Gozzi's conservatism. In pretending to reject the new genre of comic fable, Gozzi speaks through Clarice and Leandro, indirectly manifesting his own haughtiness as one who knows he is in possession of the truth and has the power of aesthetic and philosophical discernment: 'Clarice and Leandro were angry; they did not want such bumbling buffoonades and obscene rot in an enlightened century' (Gozzi 2021: 56). Gozzi would later write an entire play, *L'Augellino belverde* (*The Green Bird*, 1765, in Gozzi 1962), as a defence of counter-enlightenment ideas, but even here, his critical attitude toward the culture of the *lumières* is explicit. The Enlightenment called for reforms in all fields in which it thought necessary to debunk tradition because it had no discernible grounding in reality or reason, and such reforms, according to Gozzi, were bound to disrupt the logic of the social order.

In *Three Oranges*, the top level of that order is coded as the highest male figures in a suit of playing cards: the sovereign of the fantasy world is Silvio, *Re di Coppe* (King of Cups), and his prime minister, Leandro, is the *Cavallo di Coppe* (Knight of Cups); both are costumed as their respective figures in a deck of playing cards. This invention makes clear, in the opening scene, the relationship of *Three Oranges* to Venetian gambling culture, the ludic concept of drama on which the fiaba is based and the roles involved in its production, including that of the audience.

The centrality of gambling in Venetian social life, and thus in audience life, was the product of an entertainment industry with a long history of government-sanctioned diversions. From 1638, when the senate approved the opening of the first mercantile casino (the *ridotto*), until 1774, when all *ridotti* were officially closed, gambling, especially card games, was a distinctive feature of Venetian culture. The history of the *ridotti* runs parallel with that of the commercial theatres, the first of which, the San Cassiano, was opened only a year before the *ridotto*. In the seventeenth and eighteenth centuries, many other playing clubs opened, generally in close proximity of the commercial theatres, and the traffic between the two institutions was such that the mores they cultivated easily overlapped.

As they see the King of Cups and the Knight of Cups cross the stage, the audience immediately recognizes the playing cards to which they correspond and realizes that the players are engaging them in an imaginary game. By impersonating card figures, the actors are literally playing cards for the spectators. In the course of the first act, we learn that Fata Morgana hates the King of Cups because she lost her wealth when her hand was trumped by his card, whereas she befriends the evil Leandro because his card, the Knight of Cups, brought her luck. But on another level of interpretation, the actors are playing with spectators who likely view their spectatorship in terms of memories they have of themselves as players in a card game. In Gozzi's dramaturgical use of a card game, the Knight and the King are deployed in inimical strategies, despite the fact that they belong to the same suit. The Knight wants the crown Prince to die so that he may marry Clarice, who is next in line for the throne. At the very start of the play, then, the playwright leverages the audience's ludic imagination and familiarity with Venetian gambling culture to activate the dramatic action and to establish a playful and convivial atmosphere.

At the most elementary level, the transformation of the two-dimensional playing-card figures into three-dimensional costumes illustrates literally the principle that, on stage, the audience sees only signs of signs, which it interprets by relating them to their appropriate codes in the theatre culture of the period (Fischer-Lichte 1992: 7f). Thus, first of all, the King of Cups is a card whose function is to signal to the audience that they are about to enter into a fantasy world of serious amusement, reminiscent of gambling in the *ridotto*. The card then begins to speak and gesture as the King of an imaginary realm in which it is indeed possible for a card to be King and for another to be his disloyal minister, and the function of these signs is to raise the expectation that whatever occurs on stage is not governed by the logic of the real world. The imaginary world into which the audience crosses is one in which all sorts of magic occurrences can take place. If playing cards can signify living characters, surely other inanimate objects can do the same thing. Thus, a baker's wife, instead of expressing herself in the plebeian idiom of her class, suddenly begins to wax eloquent in sophisticated Martellian verse – two seven-syllable hemistichs separated by a medial caesura, named after the playwright and poet Pier Jacopo Martello – as do a rope, a dog and a gate hinge, effortlessly crossing the boundary that separates reality from imagination. Tartaglia and Truffaldino are astonished by what they witness, confined as they have been to a world in which such boundary crossings were considered absurdities. Like children unaware of the magician's trick, they are dumbfounded to discover that such amazing things are indeed possible. Once their imagination has been liberated, their eyes are opened, and their horizon of perception is infinitely expanded. And they thank those Martellian speakers for having so enriched their field of awareness: now they know that the ordinariness of a baker's wife, a rope, a rusty hinge and a dog can suddenly morph into the eloquence of poets. The audience, Gozzi is pleased to inform us, was delighted to see the dramatization of such wonderment.

Dramatic form

Metamorphosis can be regarded as a consequence of the fact that a sign in one code can suddenly transform into a sign of another code. In *Three Oranges*, there are two types of signs. Those of one type retain their original materiality in the transformation (e.g. the speaking rope, hinge and dog), with the consequence that the signifying activity of the second sign is incongruous with the materiality of the first, generating the humour of magic tricks. Those of the second type shed their initial materiality to acquire a new one (e.g. oranges become beautiful maidens), and their function is to send the audience's imagination into a childlike mode. Transformations presuppose the possibility of transcending the finitude of the categories of existence to which we belong and can cause us to move with ease from one realm into another. Such movement could not be achieved in reality but is the ordinary stuff of the imagination, particularly for children, whose imagination has not yet been subdued by the severity of reason. Thereby enchanted like children, Gozzi must have argued, the audience would find it easier to receive his biting criticism of literary and dramatic forms that are inimical to the apparently moribund, but in reality still vibrant, commedia dell'arte tradition.

On the opening night of *Three Oranges*, it was clear to San Samuele patrons that, despite the success enjoyed by Chiari and Goldoni, the commedia tradition represented by the Sacchi company and Gozzi was very much alive and was entering a new and exciting phase of development. The basic elements of form were mostly the same as those of traditional commedia: masked alongside unmasked characters, dramatic action shaped as a quest and a scenario for improvisation. But as is already clear from the card-like characters, there were significant innovations. Until then, in Venice, the traditional masked characters included Harlequin and Brighella in the role of young servants and Pantalone and Dottore in the role of old men, the *vecchi*. In the place of the Dottore, the pompous academic from Bologna, Gozzi's plays have Tartaglia, a dainty and colourful stutterer whose speech disorder – multiple repetition of consonants, conspicuous prolongation of vowels, splattering uncontrollably in pronouncing plosives – is the source of a type of verbal humour located at the opposite end of that associated with the Dottore's loquaciousness. Gozzi's reason for replacing the Dottore with Tartaglia in his dramatic action was entirely practical: after the death of Roderigo Lombardi in 1749, Sacchi lacked an actor trained as a Dottore, but when the talented Neapolitan actor Agostino Fiorilli joined the troupe, Tartaglia automatically became one of the masked characters. The troupe, in other words, was largely traditional but different enough to raise significant expectations of novelty in the comic actions that could be staged.

The skeletal dramatic structure of *Three Oranges* is much like that of most other commedia plays in the old repertoire: a pursuit motivated by love, hindered and aided by blocking characters and helpers, respectively, and a happy union designed to re-establish harmony and social stability. Moreover, the action exhibits the same fundamental aesthetic principle of traditional commedia: total disregard for the pseudo-Aristotelian unities of action, time and place. In particular, Gozzi flouts the unity of place, about which there was much discussion in the field. Goldoni had maintained, for example, that as long as the action took place 'in the same city and all the more so if it takes place in the same house', the rule was observed (1969: 37). In this interpretation, rather than in the narrower one of unity of place as unity of setting, he believed that it should be part of the poetics of comedy. Chiari extended unity of place to include distant cities, which is why, for narrative convenience, he could allow a character in the *Ezelino* to ride about thirty miles between scenes in order to continue having a meaningful role in the plot. Gozzi had no use either for Goldoni's effort at a liberal interpretation of the rule or for Chiari's clear violation of it.

Given the speed of ordinary modes of transportation, the disregard for unity of place might also imply disregard for the unity in time, which is to say rejection of two of the three principles with which to evaluate aesthetic merit. In *Three Oranges*, artistic merit has nothing to do with pseudo-Aristotelian rules. In the second act, Tartaglia and Truffaldino travel thousands of miles between scenes by an extraordinary means of locomotion: part of their journey is staged for the audience to see a devil blowing them forward with a bellows and then vanishing. However one conceives the dramatic action, the idea of unity of place refers to the reasonableness of locomotion within the fictional world, but only when the fictional world is constructed in analogy with the real one. A world in which magic is the major shaping force of life cannot be limited by the principles of logic. It calls on the audience to suspend disbelief by conceding the possibility of magic in all situations and at all points in time. The success of Gozzi's commedia fables shows that, when such worlds are skillfully built, audiences will readily enter them and remain there gladly for the duration of the play, as if they were children, for whom magic and fantastic wonderment are neither foolish nor incredible. In pursuing this goal, his strategy was to tap into the audience's collective memory for images and narratives that could be brought back to consciousness with delight and to intermingle them with explicit allusions to contemporary reality. This required him to find a narrative into which they could be woven as a scenario for Sacchi's players.

We do not know what the scenario of *Three Oranges* looked like, but from the author's *Reflective Analysis*, we can surmise that it was a hybrid construct, with some parts given as stage directions for improvisation and other parts in full script. Because the *Reflective Analysis* was written long after the first performance, Gozzi likely revised some details, but there is no reason to doubt his sincerity as far as improvisation was concerned. The members of the cast were, after all, the acknowledged standard-bearers of the art of impromptu performance. Consequently, we may believe that, in his first scene as the hypochondriac Prince, Agostino Fiorilli was given a summary (*argomento*) of the action and was required to improvise, both gesturally and verbally, an appropriate performance for the melancholy Tartaglia, which he did, according to Gozzi, raising a continuous roar of laughter. Gozzi reports that in the improvised scene, Tartaglia lamented the seriousness of his malady in a monologue that was both 'buffonesco e naturale' – farcical yet spontaneous. Fiorilli thus prepared the audience for Antonio Sacchi's entrance as Truffaldino, the merrymaker summoned to make Tartaglia laugh. The improvised dialogue that ensued, with Sacchi in the lead, included a dynamic exchange about the patient's illness and a medical examination by Truffaldino. Mimicking a physician, Truffaldino proceeds to the auscultation of Tartaglia's cough and performs a quality analysis of his breath and a test of his sputum – all actions that could be quickly varied by Sacchi in several iterations without tiring the audience. Truffaldino discerns in the Prince's expectorations the cause of his mawkish disposition: malodorous bits of Martellian verse, fragments of the droning metre adopted by both his rivals, Chiari and Goldoni – a fact later reflected by the verse duel in *Three Oranges*. The extempore scene ended with Truffaldino carrying by force an uncooperative Tartaglia to a balustrade on the edge of the stage, where he might see what fantastic merriment had been organized as therapy for his terrible malady. Gozzi reports that extempore scenes of this calibre, which require not only individual skill but precise teamwork – a sense elegantly and precisely captured by the word *duet*, with which John Addington Symonds, who translated Gozzi's *fiaba* into English in 1890, rendered the Italian 'scena' – could not be anything but hilarious (Gozzi 1890: 120).

Script and improvisation

When Gozzi wrote *Three Oranges*, the idea of a partly scripted scenario was not very common, although it had been in existence for about fifty years (Bartoli 1979: lxv–lxviii), and, as we have seen, was adopted even by Goldoni. Gozzi imitated Goldoni, because he too wanted to exercise control over the performance text. Significantly, Gozzi prepared a script for scenes with non-commedia characters in the so-called 'serious' roles, scenes that set the theme and propelled the narrative. But scenes involving only commedia characters, such as those featuring Tartaglia and Truffaldino, were left to the improvisatory skill of the performers. Because such extempore scenes could be quite long – Truffaldino's twenty-minute medical examination corresponds by itself to about a third of an act – skill in improvisation should not be understood only as a technical mastery of the art of performing *lazzi* and recycling old material without a script, but also as a compositional and plot-advancement ability within the narrative outline of the scenario.

The ratio of scripted to unscripted scenes in the scenario may be interpreted as a ratio of authorship to coauthorship and as an indication of the trust that the author placed in the actors for their collaborative creation of the performance text. In a metapoetic comment in the third act, Gozzi explicitly acknowledges the authorial value of the actor's contribution to the performance text and claims that, in some cases, it is superior to that of the playwright himself. Speaking about the creativity Fiorilli displayed when Tartaglia stops Truffaldino from cutting up the last of the three oranges, Gozzi states, 'In such situations, the comical masks of improvised Comedy make exaggerated physical and facial expressions, and *lazzi* that are so amusing that no ink can express or Poet surpass them' (Gozzi 2021: 62). This is very high praise indeed, not only for the members of Sacchi's troupe but for the art of commedia-style acting itself. The art of script writing has its limitations. In scenes that require a dynamic fusion of speech, gesture and movement to generate a positive aesthetic experience, it is not as creative as the art of improvisatory acting, which is also an art of impromptu composition. Here Gozzi echoes a principle of impromptu performance that was basic to the commedia dell'arte, a principle that, as we have seen, had been formulated in exceptionally clear terms by Évariste Gherardi, one of Sacchi's illustrious predecessors.

The reader of partly scripted scenarios like *Three Oranges* needs to envision a dramatic form in which scripted parts meld with improvised speech and dialogue. The fact that improvised scenes in which the performers showcase virtuosic skill in gesture and *lazzi* are most frequently used to generate laughter and that the actors at times achieve their end by misusing grammar and exaggerating their characters' poverty of speech should not blind us to the authorial significance of the players' creativity. As far as Sacchi is concerned, we know from Goldoni that he was endowed with quick understanding and a lively imagination that served him well in unscripted performance – that is, in composing text on stage within the thematic constraints of the playwright's scenario. In training himself for the task, Sacchi had become acquainted with the performance conventions of various European theatres and had made himself intimately familiar with much dramatic literature. He was conversant with the great classics of the humanist tradition to the point that in his extemporizations, one could hear clear echoes of Cicero, Seneca and Montaigne. His gestures and language were zany, sharp and full of unexpected quips and jests, but never plebeian, imbued as they were with the refinement of high culture. Sacchi was able to assimilate the elegance of that culture and to display it, even when he made use of it in comic distortions, moving the audience to laughter while satisfying their expectations with an air of freshness (Goldoni 1877: 207).

In *Three Oranges*, Gozzi makes the same point with respect to Adriana Sacchi Zannoni in the role of Smeraldina. After speaking only a hybrid of Turkish and Italian for some time, she suddenly begins to express herself with literary elegance, under the dramaturgical pretext that Fata Morgana had put 'a Tuscan devil into her tongue'. Fully conscious of her ability, she defies all poets (i.e. all playwrights) to speak (i.e. to compose) with greater literary correctness than she is doing impromptu, directly on stage (Gozzi 2021: 63). Virtuosic improvisatory performers practice their art with at least as much aesthetic elegance as playwrights. In the type of play that Gozzi proposed for the commercial theatre on the model of *Three Oranges*, scenes scripted by the playwright and scenes 'scripted' extemporaneously by performers flow seamlessly into each other as they give body to a uniform aesthetic product.

The hybrid scenario form makes such collaboration possible without reducing the actors to mere instruments of the author's ideas; however, it presents us with a difficulty concerning the ontological nature of the text as an aesthetic object. This difficulty cannot be removed by more disciplined thinking or textual research because it involves an aesthetic object that does not fit either of the two categories of textuality recognized by conventional theories of drama. But historical awareness can easily unburden us of the problem by showing us that in the commedia dell'arte tradition, in which actors routinely collaborate with playwrights in an authorial capacity in their extempore performances, hybrid textuality is an entirely legitimate and logical aesthetic concept. Unscripted commedia dell'arte exists only as performance textuality, created directly on stage by actors under the audience's gaze. Plays scripted by an author, however, can exist as both literature and performance and thus are endowed with the potential to generate two types of aesthetic experience – one in reading the author's words, and the other in viewing and hearing the performers. The hybrid textuality of *Three Oranges* fits into neither category and destabilizes both with its existence. Gozzi strategically pursued the ontological ambivalence of mixed textuality by collaborating closely with Sacchi's troupe of improvisatory players. Together, they expanded the commercial theatre's horizon of expectations in eighteenth-century Venice, marrying commedia dell'arte with fantasies from children's fables that they manipulated to generate a complex aesthetic and cognitive experience while delivering scathing criticism in an endearing form.

PART THREE

Adaptations and revivals

9

Commedia dell'arte as grotesque dance

By the first decade or so of the eighteenth century, when commedia dell'arte was well into its silver age and the careers of many actors had become noticeably unstable, some actors migrated to more genteel areas of the entertainment industry, adapting their training and talent to the requirements of new art forms, like scenic dance, either as mimes interacting with dancers or, less probably, as dancers or as consultants for the training of dancers in commedia conventions and techniques. They brought to their new art the air of festivity and aggressive laughter for which they were known, the disposition to serve the ideology of their new patrons with the docility of professionals in need of their endorsement, and the desire to show that their skills as commedia dell'arte players were worthy of the aesthetic dignity of dance.

Scenic dance, both serious and comic, was theorized and first established by the English dance master John Weaver, for whom it was not only a dramatic form of storytelling but also an art form deserving the high cultural regard enjoyed by the more established fine arts. Weaver devoted several scholarly works to the theory and history of dance, drawing on a variety of scientific, philosophical and literary sources to show that, as an art that presupposed aesthetic sensibility and generated refinement of both body and spirit, it had deep roots in the humanistic tradition and should hence be regarded as integral to any serious educational programme. The comic category of scenic dance was called grotesque dance. Weaver defined it as the dance of commedia dell'arte characters like Harlequin, Scaramouche and Pantalone. In grotesque dance, said Weaver, 'in lieu of regulated gesture, you meet with distorted and ridiculous actions, and grin and grimace take up entirely that countenance where the passions and affections of the mind should be expressed' (1728: 56; Pietropaolo 2016: 86–8). The characters embodied by grotesque dancers were unnatural characters whose physical language could be described as a purposeful distortion of the movement design of characters resembling human beings.

Lambranzi

However stylized it may have been, the movement design of commedia dell'arte dancers was understood as a deliberate warping of the language of serious dance. Serious dance was based, at least at first, on classical mythology and made use of the dignified demeanour ('regulated gesture') central to neoclassical aesthetics and courtly mores. It was elegant, stately and refined. This made it suitable for the enactment of parodies and caricatures in which all kinds of serious ideas could be treated derisively without prejudice to the gravitas that they may have had for the audience. In the early eighteenth century, the dance master who devoted much effort to such a melding of commedia dell'arte and dance was Gregorio Lambranzi, whose *Nuova scuola de' balli theatrali* (*New School of Theatrical Dancing*), was published in German and Italian in Nuremberg in 1716. Encouraged by baroque aesthetic practices, which favoured boundary crossings between the arts, Lambranzi transformed many *lazzi* into dances, providing them with the musical melody to which they should be performed and visual illustrations of the movement design the dancers were meant to imitate and execute by improvisation.

Among Lambranzi's dances, those based on the enactment of buffoonish violence and aggression, display, among other things, the dancers' ideological use of rhythmical movement without recourse to language and the aesthetic reach of which commedia dell'arte was capable in its mutated form. We can get a clear idea of the phenomenon by examining examples in which the crossing of aesthetic boundaries is also an ontological leap, since such dances usually involve a character behaving as a puppet and another as a puppeteer. Our first example depicts a shooting, a senseless attempted murder motivated only by a sudden desire to commit a violent crime – a theme whose weighty matter may have a familiar ring in our own unhappy times (Lambranzi 1966: dance n. 29–30). The scene opens with Harlequin cheerfully dancing by himself. Scaramouche approaches him with a lantern, which is a stage metaphor for darkness when the theatre is perfectly lit. The metaphor informs us that the scene takes place at night and that Harlequin is dancing alone in the dark, an ominous setting that raises expectations of impending doom. Lambranzi says that Harlequin dances in the expected manner peculiar to his character, alluding to the biomechanical range and geometric orientation of movement that constituted Harlequin's stylistic signature in the spoken theatre: the movement of an acrobatic character defined by buoyancy, skipping lightly across the stage with bouncing verticality, in opposition to the weighty and unsteady horizontal motion of the *vecchi* with whom he was frequently paired.

In Lambranzi's dance, however, Harlequin is paired with Scaramouche, who is typified by an agility of his own, though he has none of Harlequin's elatedness. Motivated by an undefined dark passion, similar to the negative feelings that he frequently embodied in spoken commedia, Scaramouche watches Harlequin for a while and then begins to mimic him dancing but suddenly stops, goes off stage to get a musket, mounts a lit candle on its barrel and fires a shot at Harlequin, who drops dead to the ground. Scaramouche then dances his way into the wings to deposit his musket, but as soon as he is out of sight, Harlequin rises uninjured and resumes his cheerful dance at the other end of the stage. Scaramouche returns to the scene of the crime and is puzzled not to find Harlequin's body where he had left it. He does not see that Harlequin, alive and well, is dancing in the darkness in another area of the stage. Scaramouche turns momentarily back, while Harlequin, suspecting that he will soon return to look for his body, stretches out in the middle of the stage, causing Scaramouche to stumble and fall over him when he returns. Scaramouche rises and tries to stand him up as an inanimate object, bends him over his knee and moves his head in various directions before loading him onto his back and walking off stage, like a hunter carrying his kill.

Representations of extreme violence and death on stage are not common in the spoken drama, on the principle that the sight of corpses would offend the audience's sense of artistic decorum. But the distancing effect of laughter, the rhythmic stylization of movement, and the aesthetic experience of music offered commedia dell'arte mimes and dancers the possibility of representing violence and death without disgruntling their audiences. Besides, all audiences of the time knew that Harlequin had always been a clown of some sort, and therefore a living theatrical being that could not really be killed, which is why he can ebulliently rise from his apparent death to return to his dance when he is alone on stage.

Objectification

When Harlequin plays dead, however, the dancer must move into a different biomechanical mode, essentially allowing another character to turn his body into a stage property for his partner. In order to play the role of an objectified character, he must allow his stage partner to move his limbs and head without offering apparent resistance, as if, in fact, Harlequin were a puppet with no volition of his own, no interior source of movement and no possibility of reacting to the external manipulation of his torso and limbs. Here Harlequin and Scaramouche in effect shift into the roles of puppet and puppeteer respectively. The scene shows commedia dell'arte entering a region of considerable aesthetic sophistication in which the boundary between living characters and lifeless objects is blurred, since the dancer performing Harlequin is required to play both. In acting like a puppet, however, Harlequin does not seek to give the impression of being a lifeless object attempting to move like a living creature, undergoing the theatrical puppet experience that Veltrusky called 'vivification', which is the normal mode of aesthetic perception elicited by puppet performances (Ambros 2012: 83). On the contrary, he pretends to be an object that was a living being only a few moments ago. Having been the victim of an attempted murder and wishing to give the impression that the attempt was successful, Harlequin becomes himself a performer and acts at having become a puppet. In this role he is an instrument of Scaramouche's signifying actions, though, unlike a real puppet, he cannot give rise to the impression of having an active consciousness independent of his puppeteer's.

The scene is constructed to draw the audience's attention from the interior life of Harlequin as a performer endowed with consciousness to the narrative being enacted. The implication of the narrative is that no real harm was done to Harlequin because he had no way of getting hurt to begin with. Harlequin's self-objectification makes him appear entirely immune to pain, and, in the larger scheme of things, violence done to such a clown-like individual matters very little, ultimately because it makes little difference even to him. The self-objectification of Harlequin becomes most meaningful in the final moment of the scene, when Scaramouche, a sinister character, always prone to intrigue and violence, suddenly mimics the role of a fine gentleman, returning from a hunting project. With this detail, the scene attenuates the violence and leaves the audience with an impression of hilarity, mixed, perhaps, with a little tenderness for the ingenuousness that motivates Harlequin to persuade Scaramouche that he is dead, and Scaramouche to equate murder with hunting. The comedy will vary with the degree of gestural silliness that the performers are capable of producing by improvisation. In performing the dance, the performer was free to vary the expressive movement details by improvisation, so long as he did not violate the constraints of the music and the narrative, while in non-musical interludes, there was considerable freedom to improvise, the only source of constraints being the narrative itself. In any case the dance was designed to confirm the view that the lower classes, represented by grotesque characters, so prone to belligerence and roguishness, are such as to benefit from the understanding of a benevolent upper class.

Similar objectification, though not self-caused, may be seen at work in scenes illustrating abusive pranks against persons rendered physically and socially vulnerable by age or injury. Such pranks produce the entertainment of seeing helpless people react histrionically in self-defence. Their dramatization illustrates to what level the cruelty of humour can be taken in acts of apparently harmless buffoonery, as they become jokes both socially acceptable and aesthetically pleasing. 'No necessary imperfection, such as old age and misfortune', wrote Richard Steele in 1715, 'shall be the object of derision and buffoonery' (1791: 215). But the normative force of his utterance may be taken as evidence that such acts of mockery were a frequent enough occurrence. Lambranzi provides us with at least two examples of the punitive attitude of society towards those suffering from the 'imperfections' to which Steele alludes. The first example is a dance in which Harlequin, fully conscious of his physical advantages, enjoys tormenting a blind man without hurting him physically. An old blind man, standing with his legs apart and supporting himself with his staff, hears music and, seized by its power, begins to sway with the upper part of his body, as if dancing without moving his feet. Harlequin approaches him from behind, crawls under his legs, grabs his hat and throws it onto his face. The blind man responds angrily, striking the air with his cane, without being able to hit Harlequin, to hilarious effect. Harlequin repeats the scene in order to elicit erratic histrionics from his victim, until he decides to put the blind man's hat on his slapstick, effectively creating another puppet character with which he taunts the blind man further. They improvise some tomfoolery and leave the stage (Lambranzi 1966: n. 32–3).

The performance of such pranks presupposes an audience with an uncharitable view of the blind and the disposition to enjoy their derision in art. From an aesthetic point of view, blindness is treated as a ruse for the performer's display of dexterity. Throughout the early modern period, blind beggars were commonly perceived as wicked and greedy scoundrels, who pretended to be destitute and begged for alms that they neither needed nor deserved, and so they were frequently denigrated in farces as objects of vilifying buffoonery (Paulson 1987: 9; Weygand 2009: ix). Lambranzi's dance is a form of high art that makes use of this tradition to generate admiration for the artist and laughter at the character. The laughter that it elicits is not the laughter of cleverness and witty remarks, but the bitter laughter of vilification, directed at the victim. The audience is in allegiance with the victimizer, who is imagined to laugh along with them (Propp 2009: 126–8). The expectation raised by the scene is that the audience will not be angered but gratified by the deftness of the performer and the cruelty of the character, who objectifies a blind man into a puppet, making him gesticulate erratically. Here Harlequin is the victimizing puppeteer rather than the victim, and the audience is in sympathy with him precisely on account of his role as victimizer. Such sympathy, however, is due to the fact that the blind man is a lower-class character. To persuade ourselves of the logic of this argument, we need only substitute the blind pauper with a blind nobleman to see that the audience would not be expected to laugh at the derision, however stylized the representation might be.

Imitation

In the early eighteenth century, the ideal objective of all the arts was still the imitation of reality, and their technical challenge was to achieve resemblance without violating the rules or leaving the materials of the art in question. This principle has a highly significant political dimension that calls for collaboration, if not outright complicity, between the arbiters of taste and the arbiters of the law. It concerns the delimitation of the aspects of reality that may or may not be imitated in each genre. In all the arts, but especially in the performing arts, the type of content to be used could be legislated directly through the policies of the boards of censors and indirectly through the budgetary approval system of the theatre's management, both of which were ultimately interpretations of the aesthetic taste and ideology of the patrons.

The patrons of commedia dancers belonged to a more genteel class than the characters in the performance. The characters might themselves occasionally assume the manners of ladies and gentlemen, but the patrons knew that the likes of Pantalone and Scaramouche were not quite in possession of the social etiquette of their class. The contrast is made especially clear by Pantalone, the character who, on account of his wealth, might find it easier than his companions to enter a higher class. Though he occasionally enjoys the activities of the more genteel classes, he still retains a foolishness that invites derision. In a scene that is metatheatrically relevant to an analysis of the intersection of dance, mime and commedia dell'arte, Pantalone goes to a dance with Pandora, but she refuses to dance with him because he is too old (Lambranzi 1966: dance n. 42). As an old man who has long had the illusion that he has the strength and sexual appeal of a youth – in Francesco Righelli's *Pantalone impazzito* (1613), we are told that he is 79 years, 11 months, 3 weeks, 4 days and 9 hours old, but has the erotic prowess of a youth – Pantalone does not take no for an answer and keeps insisting. When Pandora reaches the limit of her patience, she grips his beard and drags him in a circular dance around the stage several times before leading him into the wings.

We need not comment at length on the social situation, beyond saying that a ball, an event that has all the markings of the upper class, is a sign of the gentrification undergone by commedia dell'arte characters, who did not normally attend balls in the past. The humour of the situation, however, is not due to Pantalone's gentrification but to his age. In commedia dell'arte, the domain of movement-based buffoonery was not limited to young and agile characters like Harlequin and Scaramouche but was also available to characters of advanced years, like Pantalone, as long as the actions they performed remained within the biomechanical parameters that defined their physicality. Unlike Harlequin, who has the movement style of one whose body seems raised up by levity, Pantalone is weighed down by gravity. His kinetic space may be pictured like a pyramid described by downward vectors emanating from his head to a wide base on the stage floor around his body. He is a forward-leaning old man, with bent knees and arched back, a character with a horizontally motivated body that would fall if he were to bend it a little further, unless, of course, he shuffled his feet quickly to prevent the fall. The scene in the ballroom exploits this biomechanical characterization of old age, enabling Pandora to give the impression that she is keeping Pantalone on the verge of falling. Located at the centre in a virtually stationary position, Pandora appears to force Pantalone into performing a centripetal dance, pulling him towards her position as he tries to free himself without losing his beard. The dancers, on the other hand, are connected by Pantalone's beard only visually, and of the two it is the dancer appearing as Pantalone that gives a virtuoso performance in centrifugal dancing, pretending to pull himself away from Pandora, but dancing around her within the biomechanical constraints of old age.

Aesthetics of grotesque dance

A centripetal dance performed in a centrifugal mode requires an aesthetic design best appreciated by an audience sitting higher than the stage floor. Such a scene was likely to be more successful in Venice, in which most of the audience was in five tiers of boxes and a gallery that looked down onto the performance area, than in London or Paris, in whose theatres most of the audience was located at or below the eye-level of the performer. The architecture of multi-tiered theatres concentrated the attention of most of the audience on the 'pattern of production' (Mackintosh 1993: 135–6). From a higher vantage point, the audience would readily see that the dance was structured to give the impression that Pantalone was related to Pandora the way a puppet is related to its puppeteer, Pantalone's beard being no more than a visual metaphor for the strings with which the puppeteer controls his puppet's movement. Being a dance-within-the dance, the scene is a metatheatrical moment in which commedia characters are used by their performers to showcase the sophistication of which this mutated form of commedia was capable.

The artistry of farcical buffoonery, whether it represents aggressive or simply derisive tomfoolery, falls squarely under the general heading of the baroque aesthetic, which was then going through its own old age. In order to see this, we must view the dance, not as a cultural artefact or as a material documentation of a chapter in the history of ideas, but as an art form endowed with a peculiar type of beauty, which makes it gratifying to perception and contemplation, even when its humour is dark and its content farcical. The fine arts generally understand the baroque as an aesthetic of expansion and transgression, the result of a programme for the warping and stretching of classical conventions, on the principle that the contents to be expressed by artists included materials foreign to and larger than the artistic forms of the classical tradition. In the performing arts, this expansion required great technical skill, which soon became itself the object of display, giving rise to the phenomenon of a virtuoso performance for its own sake. In such a display, the performance erupts through the conventional aesthetic form, as if expressing something alien to it, and thereby creates its own form in the process.

Grotesque dance, however stylized it may be, has the character of such an eruption, since in the classical purview of serious dance there is no space for its deliberate distortion of conduct on the level of content and of movement design on the level of form. Yet in grotesque dance that distortion is performed with clear gestures and studied steps combined to entertain with laughter, while creating signifying patterns of movement that are easy to understand and delightful to watch. To the character's inelegant conduct, there corresponds the dancer's aesthetic embodiment of it as comic performance. The kind of aesthetic beauty involved in the art of commedia grotesque buffoonery is ultimately the beauty we discern and delight in when we see something well-structured and stylishly performed that is not in itself beautiful outside the domain of art.

A dance that represents an old man dancing may be understood aesthetically and ideologically. Aesthetically it is a performance that calls for a rhythmical stretching, arching and contorting the body beyond the degree of the posture and movement patterns that define balance and expressive elegance. It is ultimately a simulation of Pantalone's physical awkwardness, elegant in its technical precision and artistically engaging, giving the impression that the dancer may be frequently on the verge of losing his balance and collapsing. The dancer, however, has the skill to court falling down without actually doing so. Ideologically, Lambranzi makes use of dance as a paradigm for presenting a view of Pantalone designed to reveal the physical weakness of his age in an artistic and entertaining way. As an art form that requires strong, agile bodies, theatrical dance is not available to the aged. Old men who try to dance as if they were young are bound to appear clumsy, inelegant and without a sense of balance, and that is how the young dancers impersonating their roles would inevitably represent them. This is how grotesque dance contributes to the discourse on old age in contemporary culture. For the audience to view old age through the prism of dance is to see it necessarily as a perversion of decorum, both social and artistic, because, even when they are at their best, the aged appear arrogant in wanting to do something beyond their reach, foolishly making a mockery of themselves in the attempt. Grotesque dance conveys its message in the form of a delightful display of skill dramaturgically designed to give rise to an elevating aesthetic experience in which admiration for the dancer's art is inseparable from acceptance of the social discourse promoted by the dance.

10

Pulcinellate and Harlequinades

Among the different Italian terms for buffoonery, from its lightest to its heaviest form, two stand out, *pulcinellata* and *arlecchinata*, designating actions and behaviour, both on stage and in society, of the kind that might be considered typical of Pulcinella and Harlequin, the two most representative zanni of Southern and Northern commedia dell'arte respectively. In theatre scholarship, the two terms have been used to designate all manner of plays centred on Pulcinella and Harlequin, from literary dramas to improvised performances and puppet shows, generated by the migration of these and other vivacious commedia characters into adjacent areas of the entertainment industry. In a stricter sense, especially with reference to the eighteenth and nineteenth centuries, *pulcinellata* and *arlecchinata* designated sub-genres with clear-cut audience expectations concerning characters, plot, theme and performance conventions.

Pulcinellate (plural form) flourished mostly, but not exclusively, in Naples and in Rome, where the term could designate comedies and skits that showcased some aspect of Pulcinella, including always, however, his use of the Neapolitan dialect, frequently in a multilingual setting. The plots of these plays typically focused on Pulcinella but did not generally require the presence of other stock characters of the commedia dell'arte, though other conventions, including the use of standard *lazzi,* were well within the tradition of Southern commedia dell'arte. The *arlecchinata*, or harlequinade in English, developed independently abroad, especially England, with the difference that whereas in Italy and France Harlequin-centred plays were part of mainstream Northern commedia, in England they were fused with pantomime, itself with roots in commedia, and, at least in the early decades of its history, told the story without recourse to voice but with plenty of magic and special effects. Harlequinades continued to move conspicuously away from commedia dell'arte and from other scripted plays in English featuring Harlequin and other commedia stock characters. In this chapter we will turn our attention to some representative aspects of *pulcinellate* and harlequinades paying special attention to the features that mark them as distinct dramatic forms.

Pulcinellate

Plays centred on the figure of Pulcinella have a history that goes back to the early decades of the seventeenth century, but *pulcinellate* became popular in the eighteenth century, when they started to perceive themselves as a necessary counterpoint to the highbrow theatre culture of the elite. The venue that contributed most to this self-perception of *pulcinellate* was the Teatro San Carlino (1740–1884) of Naples. The elite of the city were served by the Teatro San Carlo (since 1737), where they could attend performances of operas of acknowledged musical and literary merit, in accordance with the aesthetic values of cultivated entertainment. The working classes had little or no access to this theatre world, but they developed a stage culture of their own, adopting Pulcinella as the character that could best reflect their concerns. The San Carlino, in whose name the diminutive (*-ino*) was meant to indicate the modest level of the theatre's resources but also its intent to take aim with its productions at the stateliness of the San Carlo, became the crucible in which traditional commedia elements could be brought together to generate an entertaining and aggressive *pulcinellata*. For Pulcinella was thought to epitomize the popular culture of Naples, to be, in fact, an incarnation of Neapolitanness (*napoletanità*).

For the authors of *pulcinellate*, Neapolitanness meant first of all speaking the dialect of Naples, regarded as the quintessential manifestation of its culture. Count Giacomo Marulli, a prolific nineteenth-century author of *pulcinellate* and a long-time collaborator of Antonio Petito, whose performance of the Neapolitanness of Pulcinella throughout his long career is universally recognized, published a book on his beloved dialect that may be regarded as exemplary of the complacency of its speakers. The explicit purpose of the author was to give foreigners – that is, all non-Neapolitans, other Italians included – a sense of the expressiveness (*forza espressiva*) of Neapolitan and of the grace and beauty of the ideas (*grazia e bellezza di idee*) that it can convey, in serious as well as in comic discourse, especially when it is spoken by Neapolitans of the lower social classes, to which Pulcinella belonged (Marulli 1877: 5). Such speakers use the dialect in its unspoiled purity, without any interference from foreign languages. Pulcinella may manifest his Neapolitanness in various ways, but first of all he does so by speaking Neapolitan.

The vernacular of Naples, together with Tuscan (Italian) and the other languages and dialects that occasionally intrude in it, constitutes what we may call the soundscape of *pulcinellate*, the aural background from which they emerge and which they reflect. The dominant language of the dialogue is Neapolitan, but play texts also include occasional phonemic hybrids, which are typical of multilingual settings and conventional in the commedia dell'arte tradition but sound like foreign interference to native speakers. The overt narrative function of this vernacular diversity is to generate comic stumbling blocks among characters of different backgrounds, but its dramaturgical function is to reveal the social status and cultural identity of the characters to the audience, signalling their Neapolitanness or their degree of foreignness. The heterogeneity of the soundscape manifests in Naples the same inter-ethnic dynamic that Erith Jaffe-Berg has identified in performance practices of various other cities in the peninsula, especially Mantua, where it enabled meaningful social contact and artistic collaboration both on and off the commedia stage (2015: 104). In such a soundscape, the effectiveness of vocal humour depends not only on witticisms and ludicrous statements but also on the phonological deformation of words, on improper stress, accent and vocalic gestures, that is to say on sounds that are expressive but not nomenclatural or even descriptive. As they watch the performance, the audience of *pulcinellate* also listen carefully for cultural markers of likeness and phonetic signs of otherness.

Otherness

Long before the inauguration of the San Carlino, Pulcinella fancied himself a thinker proud of being the character he was thought to be, that is a symbol of Neapolitanness. In the prologue to Verrucci's *La Colombina* (2nd edn, 1628), Pulcinella presents himself to a Roman audience by saying in Neapolitan: 'Signuri sí cha so Pulcinella, so isso cierto, anzi se non fusse me vorria pulcinellare' (Yes sir, I am none other than Pulcinella, I am he for certain, and in fact, if I were not, I would 'Pulcinellize' myself), a statement in which the reflexive neologism *pulcinellarsi* has the flavour of a proud philosophy of self-assertion (Cruciani 2004: 61). Pulcinella appears to be saying: I am indeed who I am thought to be, and I would not want to be anybody else, but if by chance I had inadvertently become somebody else, I would turn myself back into the Pulcinella that I now am. The subject pronoun in this statement is in the singular, but it could just as easily be in the plural, since Pulcinella, as a symbol of the culture, may just as well be regarded as a corporate metaphor for the people of Naples. That is, in fact, his Neapolitanness. As a character Pulcinella may evolve, of course, just as other commedia characters, the dialect and the people of Naples themselves do, but the fact that he is a symbol of Neapolitan culture at every stage of its history, that, he says, does not change.

In the commedia dell'arte repertoire, there is a *lazzo*, in which Pulcinella almost falls prey to a 'de-pulcinellization' process. It is an outrageously anti-Semitic *lazzo*, known as *scena all'ebraica*, and the process in question is circumcision, a ritual of conversion through which Pulcinella would become Jewish. The farcical circumcision is based on the *lazzo* of gelding a man, first used by Flaminio Scala in *The Pedant* (Scala 1976: 2:326) and later turned into a grotesque parody of the circumcision ritual (Baricci 2010: 136). In Filippo Cammarano's version of the lazzo in *Le cento disgrazie di Pulcinella* (*The One Hundred Misfortunes of Pulcinella*, 1824), a circumcision ritual would divest him of his Neapolitanness by turning him into a Jew and changing his name to Scialba (Cammarano 1824: 39). Pulcinella manages to escape at the last moment, preserving his personal and cultural identity. In the eighteenth and nineteenth centuries, Pulcinella's Neapolitanness included the biases of Neapolitan society with respect to outsiders, as this *lazzo* makes perfectly clear. The easiest targets to pick on were members of Jewish community, and the caricature of their perceived otherness began with their speech.

Since Medieval times, Italian Jews expressed themselves in a hybrid idiom commonly called Judaeo-Italian, in which the first term referred to words derived from biblical Hebrew and liturgical Aramaic, while the second term referred to the dialect of the particular region in which a community had settled. Judaeo-Italian was therefore a set of region-specific idioms, but the different varieties had so much in common that it is possible to speak of them, at least in the abstract, as constituting a lingua franca of the Jewish diaspora throughout the Italian peninsula. In anti-Semitic writing and performances, the salient features of this idiom were used as the verbal stuff of caricatures. For our purposes, the chief implication of this situation is that a comic skit featuring Jewish characters from one area of Italy could be performed in another area with only a minimum of adaptation. In the general tradition of the commedia dell'arte, particularly in printed *pulcinellate*, the dramaturgical denigration of Jews on stage routinely begins with a comical mimicry of Judaeo-Italian speech, focused on phonology and vocabulary.

The most conspicuous linguistic marker of ethnicity in the stereotyping of Jews consisted in exaggerated nasality. This trait was no doubt derived from a purposely distorted view of the Hebrew art of cantillation, which required a sustained nasal intonation of the biblical text. The practice led caricaturists to the depiction of Jews with big noses and exaggerated nasality. In his play, Filippo Cammarano is explicit about this, when in a stage direction he says that a group of Jews surround Pulcinella chanting 'con voce di naso e stonata', with a voice that is both nasal and out of tune (Cammarano 1824: 39). Nasality and tonality are matters of performance rather than semantics, and the performance tradition was already a sufficient stage direction for the actors impersonating the Jewish stereotypes. The printed text, however, could remind the reader of this acting convention by beginning the odd word with a nasal consonant. Thus in *Le novantanove disgrazie di Pulcinella* (*The Ninety-Nine Misfortunes of Pulcinella*) by Gregorio Mancinelli (1807 [1796]), the Hebrew moneylenders are presented as saying *Mbe!* instead of *embè!* (so what!) and *minuto* (minute) for *venuto* (come). Without a sufficiently clear context, the dialogue would be unintelligible, but it is this avoided unintelligibility that gives it a derisive charge. As for vocabulary, the caricature was constructed by the foreignness of the common vocabulary, the ease with which a word could be deformed into a mondegreen, that is a term misheard as a similarly sounding word from an unrelated speech context. Thus, in the same play (II, 12), when a Jewish character says *baruccabà*, which in Judaeo-Italian means 'welcome', Pulcinella misinterprets the salutation first as *perucca dell'abbate* ('the abbé's wig') and then as *baccalà* (literally 'salt cod', but figuratively 'idiot'), adding one incongruity to the other.

The scene between Pulcinella and the Jewish characters is replete with strange sounding Judaeo-Italian words, like *zagú, mengoti, zuimmi* (all meaning money) and *sciurisciati* (confusion), and comic mispronunciations of Italian and dialect that mark the cultural foreignness of the speakers. Such markers of foreignness are designed to reach the audience as intrusions of minority languages into the phonetic transparency of their own. Longstanding members of the community, represented by Pulcinella and other local characters, speak to each other in Italian and Neapolitan without drawing attention to the acoustic materiality of their utterances, which are for them invisible carriers of thought. But when outsiders attempt to enter their community, language loses its transparency, as the encounter is temporarily refocused on the vocal substance of mispronounced words and mysterious linguistic hybrids. In the cultural community of *pulcinellate*, language is both a crucial test of an outsider's capacity for invisible integration in the community and the community's instrument of cultural alienation. Linguistic opacity is frequently used as a theme of minority dramaturgy to degrade the culture of characters trapped in their ethnic alterity. The comic effect of the caricatures employed in such a dramaturgy is itself dependent on the presence of a complicit audience, equally inimical to the satirized community and conditioned by the same distorted perception of its alterity. The dramaturgy of *pulcinellate*, in other words, is rooted in and reflects the ethnic biases of the community that it serves.

Vocal expression and humour

The poetics of vocal humour involves a dialectical interplay between two characters who continue to misinterpret each other's utterances. They take turns in perceiving each other as speaking in absurdities, taking perfectly clear words as mondegreens, or words that they think they hear instead of the words that were actually uttered. The dialogue proceeds through a series of comical equivocations. Thus in scene 2.1 of Mancinelli's *Le novantanove disgrazie di Pulcinella*, the innkeeper mishears Pulcinella's *notte* (night) as *botte* (wine barrel), his *passaggiere* (traveller) as *pasticciere* (pastry baker), *minestra* (soup) as *finestra* (window) and so on with several partly rhyming or similarly sounding words, generating a nonsensical exchange as a succession of quick misinterpretations. Unaware of his own deafness, the innkeeper says that Pulcinella must be deaf to mishear so many of his words! Such scenes cannot be very long because they do not contribute much to the plot. Their function is primarily aesthetic, that is they are no more than a series of jokes designed to promote laughter by the incongruity of utterance and interpretation in the style of verbal *lazzi*.

A significant type of linguistic humour is produced by cacographies, or intentionally comic misspelling of words without altering their basic pronunciation. For example, in speaking French, Pulcinella may be represented in the text as saying *monsiù*, which uses Neapolitan as a phonetic language to approximate the sound of French *monsieur*. The intent is to give the reader the double impression that Pulcinella is less than literate in French and that the audience would hear the French word pronounced with a distinct Neapolitan accent. The interest that cacography has for students of commedia dell'arte tradition is that it concerns the text both as a work of literature, with episodes of humour addressed to the eye of the reader, and as a script for an actor, in which case a cacography may be regarded as a stage direction for the performance of the character's illiteracy in attempting to speak the language, or to adopt a stylistic register beyond his competence. In scenes of this type, characters are frequently used by the playwright as instruments of parody meant to bring highbrow language down to the level of a rustic vernacular, giving rise to a comedy of degradation laden with ideological significance.

In *pulcinellate* of the nineteenth century, cacography is routinely used in an aesthetic of parody. A good example of this is Antonio Petito's comedy *Na bella Elena, bastarduta nfra lengua franzesca, toscana e napoletana* (*The Beautiful Helen Bastardized Between the French, Tuscan and Neapolitan Languages*, 1869), written and produced as a parody of Offenbach's opera *Belle Hélène* (1864), which had become popular among the cognoscenti of high culture in Naples. Since *Belle Hélène* was itself a comedy, Petito made use of low-class comedy to parody high-class comedy. Pulcinella is a lowly member of a troupe of travelling players who are asked to perform, in an inn near Naples, Offenbach's *Belle Hélène* pretending to be a French-speaking company. The mayor, who fancies himself French-speaking but knows that his knowledge of the language is not perfect, has always a dictionary on hand to look up new words, though he can be easily fooled by an actor mimicking a native French speaker. In the text we encounter many words like *disgiunè* (for *déjeuner*, 26) and expressions like *Monsiu Pulsin* (*Monsieur Pulcinella*, 31) together with other hybrid formations which, when inserted into perfectly correct grammatical structures, give rise to a confusing dialogue that has the rhythm of comprehensible speech but is very difficult to interpret.

In a brief metatheatrical moment, the mayor suggests in Neapolitan that to make sense of such situations of incomprehension one has to recognize that there are three linguistic codes at work in the scene's Babelian medley. He says: 'mme pare che chiste stanno parlanno no poco Francese, no poco Taliano, e n'atro ppoco Napolitano' (it seems to me that they are talking a little in French, a little in Italian and a little in Neapolitan, 41). Yet that recognition cannot be enough for the audience to understand every part of the dialogue. As the stage directions make plain, an aria sung on stage must sound French but must actually be a parody of the language (43), and the French spoken by the actors in dialogue must be unintelligible (45), despite the fact that the audience may nonetheless understand what is going on.

These observations about *Na bella Elena* are applicable, with minimal variation, to other *pulcinellate*, in which the main characters' sense of language loyalty is very profound and in which there are occasional scenes that foreground loyalty as a theme against the soundscape of a multilingual city. The aesthetic appeal of such scenes is the appeal of a text that expresses much more by the flow of its sound than can be signified by its individual segments. The occasional episode of semantic obscurity is deliberate; it is an essential part of the aesthetic form of a text for an audience that is complacent about the expressiveness of its own language, to which it anchors its identity as a cultural community, as in early commedia.

FIGURE 9 *Pulcinella telling stories, engraving, Italy, nineteenth century. (Photo by DeAgostini/Getty Images.)*

Harlequinades

In the *arlecchinate* of the same period, there are no parallel themes of language loyalty. There are at least two good reasons for this: the first is historical and concerns the nature of Harlequin as a character. Unlike Pulcinella, Harlequin is not a native citizen of the city with which he is normally associated in the eighteenth century, namely Venice. He is an immigrant *zanni* from Bergamo, a distant and depressed corner of the Republic of Venice. In the city of Venice, he is very much an outsider who tries to fit in as best he can, learning to speak Venetian, though, at least according to Brighella in Goldoni's *Servant of Two Masters*, he has been unable to get rid of his thick accent and mannerisms, which make his otherness stand out: 'nol sa gnanca parlar' (he can't even talk properly, III.5). The second reason is aesthetic, and it has to do with the genre's privileging of visual to aural discourse. Just as *pulcinellate* rely heavily on the aural dimension of culture, exploiting the dramatic potential of noise, confusion and what we called linguistic opacity, *arlecchinate* count chiefly on the semiotic potential of visual culture to communicate their plot and message to the audience. Thus costumes, mime and dance took immediate precedence over dialogue in the conception of new *arlecchinate* from the early eighteenth century on.

There was, of course, some overlap with *pulcinellate* in the choice of *lazzi* and plot material, as was to be expected in an international entertainment market in which many companies were on tour for a good part of the year. The commedia dell'arte *lazzo all'ebraica*, for example, was performed in 1726 at the King's Theatre in Haymarket by a company featuring Harlequin rather than Pulcinella with a scenario called *Harlequin's Misfortunes or his marriage interrupted by Brighella's cunning, with his comical circumcision* (London, 1726). But this is not the direction in which the *arlecchinata* developed, especially in England, where it soon began to move away from commedia dell'arte and come closer to pantomime. Eventually, Harlequin was fully absorbed by English pantomime, while the performer embodying him was given a new artistic mandate, in accordance with the aesthetic goals of his new genre. After 1717, when the term harlequinade was first used to describe a pantomime centred on Harlequin, the terms pantomime and harlequinade were considered synonymous names for this category of dramatic art (Toepfer 2019: 441).

In England, the theatres most closely associated with the early development of the harlequinade as a visual dramatic form were Drury Lane and its competitor Lincoln's Inn Fields, respectively under the direction of John Weaver and John Rich. Weaver invented the genre as short interludes separating the acts of serious narrative dances. Rich, also known by his stage name of Lun, introduced stage machinery for the creation of spectacular effects, made Harlequin more acrobatic, redesigned his costume as a form-fitting body suit and gave him a magic bat or slapstick of sorts with which to cause miraculous transformations. The other characters were also distanced from the commedia dell'arte. Pantaloon derived from old Pantalone, the character most closely associated with the city of Venice and its dialect, lost his Venetian heritage to become a miserly old man, forbidding the union of Harlequin and Columbine. Columbine, who was a maidservant to Pantalone's daughter, became Pantaloon's daughter or ward. Pierrot, who was newly cast as an utterly witless valet, was originally an elegant *zanni* of endearing simplicity by the name of Pedrolino. Clown, an aide to Pantaloon in the latter's effort to chase Harlequin away from his daughter, no longer has anything in common with the commedia dell'arte Pagliaccio.

Simultaneously with this naturalization of the main characters, there was a simplification of commedia dell'arte plot material, which was reduced to the theme of Harlequin's forbidden love for Columbine. The artistic mandate received by performers entering the arena of harlequinades included the use of a more precise gestural language, unambiguous with respect to reference and clear in its representation of narrative flow, since, unlike Italian plays centred on Harlequin, harlequinades belonged to a genre of non-verbal performances. The mandate also included playing a Harlequin that could exhibit a more refined behaviour, especially in romantic pursuits, since in the naturalization process he became somewhat gentrified. Most of all, it included performing in an artistic ethos of spectacular metamorphosis, since, in its incorporation of tales of magic, the harlequinade made increasing use of supernatural forces and transmutations as well as other special effects.

Harlequinade innovations

At different points in the long history of the harlequinade, one can discern significant developments. Its internal dynamics changed under the pressure of the aesthetic orientation of producers in control of the theatre and of the special skills of the actors impersonating the characters. Among the comic interludes developed at Drury Lane, a highly significant innovation was the creation of the character of Harlequine by the talented dancer and actress Hester [Santlow] Booth. This is the first appropriation by a British actress of a male commedia dell'arte character (Miller Lewis 1999: 84). In Italian commedia dell'arte we occasionally come across an Arlecchina, but only as a variant of Colombina and not as a female Harlequin (Nicoll 1976: 97; Radulescu 2012: 85). But Harlequine was actually a female version of Harlequin, a female character that had all his male attributes minus his gender. Hester Booth's performance was not a form of cross-dressing, in which an actress in breeches impersonates a male character – there is no evidence that the actress performed a male Harlequin in breeches (Fowler 2010, p. 47) – but the performance by a woman of a male character whose gender had already been reconstructed as female in the scenario. Nor was it a case of theatrical hermaphroditism, since only the character's female gender was impersonated, though through that gender the audience saw also the male attributes

FIGURE 10 *Hester Booth, by John Ellys, London, Victoria and Albert Museum (via Wikimedia Commons, public domain).*

of Harlequin as if they had been appropriated by the female character. In the audience's perception of Harlequine, the two genders interact continuously in a sophisticated aesthetic of cross gendered identity (Miller Lewis 1999: 84).

Another significant innovation centred on the character of Harlequin was brought about by David Garrick when he assumed the direction of Drury Lane (1747). Although he was not in sympathy with the pantomime aesthetic as it had been developing to his day, he wrote a pantomime himself, *Harlequin's Invasion* (1759–60), in which, among other things, he catered to the growing taste for extravagant wizardry and special effects, and reintroduced dialogue, having realized that pantomime artists of the calibre of Lun were not easy to come by. A further notable change occurred when Joseph Grimaldi reconceived the character of Clown, giving him a more flamboyant costume, and altered the standard plot situation by enlarging his role in Pantaloon's rush against Harlequin. These kinds of development continued to increase the distance between harlequinades and commedia dell'arte, until they had nothing in common other than the names of some characters.

In the early nineteenth century, the uniqueness of the English pantomime was recognized by contemporary French and Italian playwrights, who occasionally imitated the form in their own languages. For example, *L'orang-outang ovvero l'uomo del bosco incivilito* (*The Orangutan or the Civilized Man of the Forest*, 1806), is an Italian version of a French pantomime scenario composed by Édouard-Alexandre Bignon. It was offered as an imitation of an English pantomime, 'imitata dagli Inglesi', as is explicitly declared on the title page. In the introduction to the Italian text, the author or the translator – we are not told who wrote it – defines English pantomimic harlequinade as a comedy of gestures that speaks only to the eyes of the audience (5, 10) and adds that, like architects who use the bricks of an old building to raise a new one in a different style, the authors of English pantomime scenarios took characters from the commedia dell'arte – Harlequin, Columbine and Pantalone in the principal roles – and created a new dramatic form which had no need for speech. Conspicuous as it was in conventional commedia dell'arte, and even more so in Neapolitan *pulcinellate*, vocal aurality had no relevance for pantomimic harlequinade in the English style, which was a visual art of the stage.

The introduction to *L'orang-outang* considers the salient features of the harlequinade form under the influence of its first champion, John Weaver, re-sketching in a few broad strokes his derivation of scenic dance from ancient Roman pantomime, which he raised to a higher level of artistic dignity. The introduction explicitly refers to the precise gestural vocabulary of English pantomime dancers – subtle in its expressiveness, precise in its meaning, and untainted by any of the lubriciousness that the body language of pantomimes had in

Roman antiquity. In entering this domain from the commedia dell'arte, Harlequin had to shed off his most uncouth habits and curb his inclination to tomfoolery. In the process, he also honed his skills as a trickster and rose a little from his base instincts to discover the power of sentiment and romance, all in a more refined manner than he had been accustomed to in his earlier existence. In the plays of his own country, Harlequin had his eye on the female servant, who was his counterpart Columbine, and would never dare entertain the thought of aiming higher than that. In English pantomime, however, he pursues a different Columbine, who is Pantalone's daughter rather than her maid, violating a basic convention of commedia dell'arte concerning character relations and transgressing a basic social norm of the time. In their pantomimes, we read in the Italian introduction to *L'orang-outang*, the English have given Harlequin a much higher social ambition than he could ever aspire to in the genre of his origin and in the culture of his native country.

11

Commedia dell'arte in the opera libretto

Commedia dell'arte performances are both visual and aural, and while the visual dimension, consisting of colourful costumes, masks, gestures and movement, has been frequently commented upon throughout history, the significance of its aural dimension has been made the subject of rigorous study and reflection much less frequently. Based on the Horatian principle that we expresses the emotions of the soul by the way we use language (*Ars poetica* 111), in his treatise on *Acting from Memory and by Improvisation* Perrucci goes through the different alterations of the voice that performers should make when they deliver their speeches, allowing the sounds they produce to exercise the semiotic function of revealing personality and attitudes in ways that neutral speech could not do (Perrucci 2008: 54). In their performances, commedia dell'arte actors made use of literary Italian, several vernaculars, linguistic blends of foreign languages, vocal gestures, volume and pitch alterations, together with mechanical sounds from noise-making props as well as music from song and instruments – a large plurality of aural signifiers, several of which were received by the audience in simultaneous perception. Behind this semiotic complexity is the linguistic heterogeneity of Italy and the sonorous richness of the orality in which the audience lived, frequently relying on visual body language and gestures, but also on intonation, vocal gestures and inarticulate sounds to grasp the meaning of indistinct and unfamiliar words. This orality penetrated into literary works and served as the semantic base of texts that purported to sound like speech. In the text the naturalness of sound could be identified as a scripted residue of the living oral culture (Henke 2002: 31f). It is obvious that in a performance, not all verbal signifiers pronounced on stage could be equally intelligible to the audience, whatever degree of familiarity they may have had with the regional vernaculars of Italy other than the one in which they themselves were immersed.

The meaning of indistinct phrases said on stage was made immediately clear, however, by the communicative force of facial gestures and non-verbal acoustic elements. Considered under its sonic aspect, a commedia performance could be regarded as a 'continuum of meaningful aurality', as Emily Wilbourne terms the acoustic materiality of the genre (2016: 20). In this continuum, commedia reveals itself as a dramatic form in which the meaning of its often indistinct verbal text is made plain by various acoustic signifiers, each reinforcing the other by osmosis and compensating with its own expressive power for the blurriness of unfamiliar words and phrases, in a manner designed to leave the audience with an impression of the naturalness of speech imitated on stage. This acoustic continuum of signifiers gave commedia dell'arte the potential to cross with relative ease the conceptual boundary that separated it from other dramatic forms with differently organized sonic heterogeneities, most notably opera, which emerged as a distinct theatrical genre at the turn of the sixteenth century.

The connection between commedia dell'arte and opera, first brought to the attention of modern scholarship by the noted musicologist Nino Pirrotta (1955), has been a frequent object of study, especially concerning the period subsequent to the waning of commedia dell'arte. The hybrid form created by the permeation of commedia dell'arte into the domain of serious music occurs in madrigal comedy, a genre from the immediate prehistory of opera, but it continued in conspicuously greater measure throughout the history of opera, particularly after the establishment of opera buffa as a distinct form in the early eighteenth century. Some commedia scenarios were transformed directly into librettos, while other librettos frequently borrowed from mainstream commedia scenes of dramatic action, usually inserting them in the recitatives and, less frequently, in duets, which allowed for more action than arias.

But the strongest connection concerns the audience, for the first audiences of the musical theatre were familiar with commedia dell'arte performances. By the time that opera came into being, theatre audiences had been accustomed by commedia players to the idea that characters had identities as sonic types. Much like their costumes, the sounds associated with individual characters – melodiousness of speech flow, intonation, loudness, speech defects, mechanical noises – constituted sonic profiles that conveyed essential information about them, such as their regional origin and inherent behavioural inclination, all the while raising expectations about the kinds of phrases they were likely to insert into their speeches in any given situation. Familiarity with the sonic profiles of different character types gave the audience the ability to grasp with precision meaning couched in indistinct language, to predict some aspects of the form and content of speeches and to experience the aesthetic pleasure of expectedness. Such familiarity was a basic assumption of early operas as well, which counted on the audience's ability to perceive meaningful sounds, linguistic as well as paralinguistic, particularly in the appreciation of recitative as a coded form of the naturalness of speech. It was mostly through its education of theatre audiences to auditory perception, but also through the habituation by librettists to the idea of sonic profiles, that commedia dell'arte first penetrated the domain of opera in a profound way. Given the facilitative function of aurality, the transition of the spoken dramatic form to the musical one, as Wilbourne has brilliantly argued (2016: 153), was not such a leap as one might otherwise imagine.

Commedia dell'arte scenes in
Don Giovanni

At the level of general conception of the dramatic form, the leap appears larger than it was also because the presence of commedia dell'arte themes and *lazzi* in famous operas is not always easy to discern, despite their deep roots in scenarios and in the performance tradition of mainstream commedia. A notorious case in point is Mozart's and Lorenzo Da Ponte's *Don Giovanni*. Among the scenarios that served as matrices of librettos, one of the most famous, which circulated in various versions, was *Il convitato di pietra* (*The Stone Guest*), originally based on *El burlador de Sevilla* by the Spanish playwright and priest Gabriel Téllez, better known as Tirso de Molina. Following a long period of metamorphosis through different dramatic forms, the story re-emerged most spectacularly as Mozart's and Da Ponte's *Don Giovanni*. As is well known, there are two versions of the opera, one first produced in 1787 in Prague and the other in 1788 in Vienna. Both versions are indebted to the commedia dell'arte, but the second more so than the first.

The version of the opera that is normally produced in modern times, however, is a dramaturgical composite of the first and second versions, conflated by conductors into a single text on the basis of aesthetic criteria. The amalgamation of the two editions comes usually with some structural rearrangement of the material and always with the excision of three commedia-type scenes from the second version (Act II scenes 11–13), scenes of physical drama judged to be alien to the true aesthetic nature of the opera, Mozart's and Da Ponte's own judgement notwithstanding. In performances of *Don Giovanni* textual philology and textual dramaturgy are dominated by the aesthetic taste of musicologists and conductors rather than original manuscripts. To quote a famous example, the distinguished musicologist Alfred Einstein wrote that in the 1788 version Mozart 'positively ruined the second act' (1938: 417), so illogical and out of place did the scenes of commedia dell'arte physicality appear to him.

The physical drama of the expunged scenes is an example of commedia dell'arte buffoonery. Zerlina enters the playing area gripping Leporello by his hair with one hand and brandishing a knife with the other. She drags him around the stage, all the while making menacing gestures at him as he asks for pity. A peasant enters the stage and helps Zerlina subdue Leporello so that she may tie his hands with a kerchief. She forces Leporello to sit on a chair and ties him down with a rope before tying the chair to a window frame. In the accompanying recitative, Leporello, fearing the worst, asks for mercy, which Zerlina angrily denies, saying that she intends to pull out his hair, cut off his head, carve out his eyes, pull out his heart and feed it to the dogs, which she would also like to do with Don Giovanni's heart. In a duet following the physical action, Leporello laments his fate at her hands, while she says that she feels her heart light up with joy as she does what she is doing, because this is what men like him deserve. Zerlina leaves the stage to fetch Donna Elvira and Masetto, leaving Leporello by himself for a brief time. Alone on stage, Leporello struggles to free himself, but in the attempt he tears down the window frame and heads for the exit, dragging both the chair and the window frame behind him.

Zerlina's punitive stance on men who mistreat women is reminiscent of the feminist posturing of Smeraldina in the commedia dell'arte tradition, in which, as in Goldoni's *Servant of Two Masters* (II.8), she speaks with passion of the undeserved bad reputation of women and of the true lack of fidelity in men. As a character, Zerlina belongs to the Smeraldina character type, but the vehemence and the indignation with which she speaks are probably unprecedented. They are, however, fully consonant with the punitive physicality of the scene, which is strongly reminiscent of commedia farcical traditions in every detail. Zerlina's dragging of Leporello around the stage, for example, may have been consciously patterned on the *lazzo*, turned into a dance by Gregorio Lambranzi, in which Pandora, like a puppeteer, forces Pantalone to dance around the stage, handling him by his beard. The only variant in Da Ponte's version is that a beard has been replaced by hair, but the rest of the *lazzo* is the same. Zerlina goes as far as to hint at the fact that this particular bit of theatrical physicality belongs to the dance version of the commedia dell'arte. She tells Leporello that she will show him just how 'the dance' will end, 'vedrai come finisce il ballo' (Da Ponte 1990: 423). As in Lambranzi's dance version of the *lazzo*, the male performer has the virtuosic task of moving around the stage while giving rise to the impression that he is being dragged by his female partner who uses his hair the way a puppeteer uses his strings.

This *lazzo* is an example virtuosic buffoonery, which, together with the other physical drama in the expunged scenes, linked the Vienna 1788 version of the opera, intentionally and in a very conspicuous way, to the dramaturgical conventions of the commedia dell'arte. These conventions were brought into the opera by Mozart and Da Ponte as an integral part of the aesthetic vision that *Don Giovanni* was meant to express to the Viennese audience. The removal of these scenes is the result of an aesthetic clean-up of the opera by conductors and musicologists, presumably on the principle that an opera worthy of Mozart and Da Ponte should not include any traces of broad commedia dell'arte. Such traces would surely spoil the aesthetic purity of the rest, whether or not they were authored and put there by the composer and librettist themselves.

The intransigence of modern aesthetic criteria, based on a less heterogeneous view of the opera, do not concern the presence of motifs whose dramaturgical origins as commedia dell'arte conventions are no longer easy to discern. A case in point, perhaps the most notorious in the entire opera, is Leporello's catalogue aria 'Madamina il catalogo è questo', in which Leporello displays to Donna Elvira the long list of Don Giovanni's conquests, enumerating them by geographical origin and physical traits. This aria has deep roots in the Neapolitan commedia dell'arte, where it originated as a *lazzo*. It was in Naples that Tirso da Molina's play was first produced in Italy. It so happened that, in the general perception of Neapolitan performers and audiences, the resident Spanish Viceroy of the Kingdom of Naples was a libertine who liked to boast about his sexual exploits and who, in various other regards, belonged to the character type of Don Giovanni. This inspired the composition of a *lazzo* focused on the image of a catalogue of conquests. In the scenario *Il convitato di pietra* in the Casamarciano collection, we read that Don Giovanni, after telling Tisbea that she should feel honoured that he has taken his pleasure with her, asks Pulcinella to put her name at the top of the list of his conquests, which Pulcinella promptly does and throws the list at her, causing her to jump into the sea to drown herself (*Casamarciano*, vol. 1, 425). Throughout the seventeenth century, the *lazzo* acquired complexity and momentum, appearing in other urban centres in slightly different forms and with different dramaturgical purposes. For example, Domenico Biancolelli, the distinguished Harlequin of the Italian troupe in Paris, used it to generate audience participation. He recounts that, having dangled the catalogue before Don Giovanni's most recent conquest, he unrolled it and threw it onto the audience in the parterre, inviting the spectators to see whether the names of the women in their families were to be found in the list (Biancolelli 1978: 139). The *lazzo* was included with different theatrical gestures in several other versions of the story on the commedia dell'arte stage, in both scenario and scripted form (Megale 2020: 301–3), until, with Da Ponte and Mozart, it morphed into the famous aria.

Commedia elements in *Ariadne Auf Naxos*

In many respects *Ariadne auf Naxos* dramatizes how, in the imagination of a composer and a librettist, commedia dell'arte can enter the domain of opera without sacrificing the theatrical identity of its characters, who undergo little or no adaptation beyond gaining the ability to express themselves musically. For this reason, the 1916 edition of *Ariadne auf Naxos*, which is considerably different from the 1913 edition, is of interest to students of the dramatic forms of the commedia dell'arte. A metatheatrical work, *Ariadne auf Naxos* tells the story of how an opera seria and a harlequinade, originally meant to be performed sequentially by different troupes, were amalgamated and performed as a single work, by order of the Viennese patron who commissioned this peculiar form of entertainment for the pleasure of his dinner guests. The opera was indeed of a serious kind: the disconsolate Cretan princess Ariadne was abandoned on the island of Naxos by her beloved Theseus, and there she suffered until the arrival of Bacchus, whom she ended up marrying. The island, however, is also the place where a travelling commedia dell'arte troupe has just arrived, and so the actors participate in the dramatic action. The commedia actors did not have, nor did they need, a script, being, as the Dance Master says standing outside the drama (Hofmannsthal 2017: 14), experts in the art of improvisation, players who can see their way through any situation in which they may find themselves ('Diese Leute wissen zu improvisieren, finden sich in jede Situation').

The opera-within-the-opera is set before a cave in front of which Ariadne intones her lament, while the five commedia characters – Zerbinetta, Scaramouche, Truffaldino, Brighella and Harlequin – at first watch unseen and then try to console her. Zerbinetta, who is Ariadne's commedia counterpart, is a woman of the world who knows a thing or two about faithless men and about the resiliency of forsaken women. She knows well that a woman abandoned by her lover on a desert island – which, she says, could be anywhere – will go on lamenting her fate until another handsome suitor comes along to sweep her off her feet. In the meantime, she and her companions do their best to comfort Ariadne with their antics and improvisations, introducing a touch of contextual lightness around Ariadne's lachrymose performance. In her famous aria, *Großmächtige*

Prinzessin (*Oh great Princess*), which is a list of love affairs
in the manner of Leporello's catalogue aria, she tries to give
Ariadne a hint of the countless instances in which she allowed
men to believe they had seduced her. Zerbinetta also says that
she too has known despair, but has picked herself up each time
without difficulty.

From this brief sketch of *Ariadne auf Naxos,* we can
immediately see how the commedia dell'arte could enter into
another genre and how it can become involved in its narrative
and yet remain what it was independently, except for its
adoption of song as the medium of expression. Richard Strauss
and Hugo von Hofmannsthal, who took a particular interest in
dramatic forms of various kinds, overcame all dramaturgical
discordance between the aesthetic form of a commedia dell'arte
play, with its expected caricatural and parodic purport, and the
sombre seriousness of an opera of lament, by transforming the
contrast into a lyrical interplay of comedy and sentiment. In
this dramaturgy of coquetry and tenderness, the expression of
light sentiment and wry humour move lightly in counterpoint,
attenuating each other's normal effect in the process and
creating a new type of aesthetic experience.

Ferruccio Busoni's *Arlecchino*

In our next example, Ferruccio Busoni's *Arlecchino oder Die
Fenster*, we can see how such a melding can occur without
adopting song as the medium of expression. In his *Sketch of
a New Esthetic of Music* (1917), the composer suggests that
an artistic tradition is like a plaster mask taken from a living
model. Different generations of artisans make the mask their
own, as a form they can use in their own art. They thus give it
an expressive function that is consonant with their own artistic
temperaments and perhaps alter some of its details in response
to the aesthetic promptings of their times. At all stages of the
transmission-and-reuse process, however, the mask retains

the basic form of its prototype, in virtue of which its new incarnation is recognizable as an aesthetic interpretation of the original. The resemblance of the new version to the prototype may no longer be determined with clarity by an artist, having become 'largely a matter of imagination' (Busoni 1962: 77), but its consilience with the original is nonetheless understood to be there at all times, wherever the artist's imagination may take what it receives from history.

The parallelism helps us to see how generations of artists can bring innovations into a tradition, injecting new life into it, without feeling that they are betraying its fundamental principles. Busoni's treatment of the commedia dell'arte in his one-act opera *Arlecchino oder Die Fenster*, first performed in Zurich in 1917, is a case in point. The opera, for which Busoni wrote the libretto as well as the music, is organized as a sonata in four movements. In each, Arlecchino is cast in a different role: a scoundrel in the first, a soldier in the second, an unfaithful husband in the third and an unscrupulous lover in the fourth. At the structural level, the most conspicuous commedia dell'arte feature of the opera is the fact that Harlequin is a speaking character, who recites his part in rhythmic speech while the other characters sing theirs. Arlecchino is a masked character of the spoken drama, and it is as such that he is included in the opera. Opposite him, however, cast as his wife in the third movement, Colombina sings her part. Reacting against the then dominant conception of opera as a continuous flow of song and instrumental music, Busoni structures the libretto of his *Arlecchino* as an amalgamation of speech and song, with his title character taken directly from the commedia dell'arte tradition, speaking and gesturing in the manner of the spoken drama.

This importation of spoken commedia into the domain of opera is a general feature of Busoni's aesthetics, in which episodes of the theatrical, literary and musical heritage are given conspicuous presence by way of allusion, quotation or adaptation. In addition to a speaking Arlecchino, the first movement of the opera, includes Matteo del Sarto, holding

the *Divine Comedy* in his hands and singing the famous
lines in which Francesca tells Dante how, while she and her
brother-in-law Paolo were reading the romance of Lancelot
and Guinevere, they became emotionally entangled in the
story to the point that they were seized by a sudden passion
for one another and committed adultery, for which they were
consigned to hell for eternity. While Matteo sings his reading
of Dante in the foreground, the audience watches Arlecchino
kissing Annunziata, Matteo's beautiful wife, through a
window in the background. The lines of poetry that he has
just read inspire Matteo to think of operatic melodies, and just
as he expresses this sentiment, the orchestra begins to sound
the champagne aria from Mozart's *Don Giovanni*. The music
is heard by the audience as if it resonated in the character's
imagination, while Arlecchino and Annunziata continue to
mime their erotic encounter at the window. Arlecchino then
jumps out onto the street, momentarily waxing lyrical himself
with Francesca's last words to Dante, which he addresses to
Matteo: 'quel giorno piú non vi leggemmo avante' (*Inferno*
5.138), or that day we read no further. While overtly about
illicit love, the Francesca episode is also about the dangers of
emotionally involved reading, and this aspect of the story is
emphasized by Busoni.

From the scene just described, we can see how Busoni made
use of the commedia dell'arte and what innovations he brought
to it. The scene lends itself to this observation: contrary to the
aesthetics of realism, here the audience is not meant to identify
with the characters – not with Matteo, who is an admirer of
Dante but an easily deceived husband, nor with Harlequin,
who, though a cheerful rogue, is a despicable deceiver. The
text prompts the audience to identify instead with the author.
It does so by depicting a scene consisting of theatrical, literary
and musical segments, and by engaging them as commentaries
of each other. The recognition of this structure has the effect
of distancing the spectators from each segment of narrative to
look at it from the perspective of the other segments, which is
what the composer does in layering them. Working together,

these different segments tell a complex story, but singularly they each act as distancing devices designed to undermine emotional involvement with the story itself and psychological identification with the characters. Thus, Arlecchino's and Annunziata's scene of mimed lovemaking visually undermines any feeling of intellectual sympathy that a member of the audience may have for Matteo as a reader of sublime poetry, while the echo of *Don Giovanni* musically subverts Matteo's inspired reading of Dante by reminding the audience that, ironically, Francesca ended up in hell for identifying too closely with the lovers of the story that she was reading. At the same time, the scene is a reminder that, although not in hell at the moment, Arlecchino has a demonic antecedent in him, Alichino being the name of one of the devils in Dante's *Inferno* (22.125).

Hell is what Francesca, Harlequin and Don Giovanni have in common. Yet in Matteo's reading of it, the story cited from Dante may be easily seen as denunciation of both Harlequin and Don Giovanni, who can know nothing of the passion for which Francesca suffers in hell. Busoni's opera is a complex play of ironies and aesthetic reflection, a drama in which tragic and comic elements are brought together visually, musically and poetically, to invite the audience to respond to the text intellectually rather than emotionally. It calls for a sophisticated aesthetic sensitivity that is a far cry from the simple openness to broad humour that Harlequin demanded of the audience in the early commedia dell'arte tradition.

12

Continuity and transformation in the twentieth century

On 22 November 1989, Giorgio Strehler was awarded an honorary doctorate by the University of Toronto in recognition of his enduring contribution to world theatre. In his convocation address, Strehler gave a synoptic outline of his theory of the theatre, and among the topics that he discussed was the staging of plays written in the distant past. He observed that the production of a play is a collective rewriting of the text, using the current semiotic codes of the theatre and society, by all those involved in staging it under the coordination of the director, whose task it is to enable the text to become meaningful to the audience. Play production is neither a philological nor an archaeological operation. It does not seek to discover and bring forth for inspection the exact meaning of a dramatic text in the historical context in which it was produced. It seeks rather to establish a link between the author and the audiences of today. A play is neither the dead artefact of an archaeologist nor the unadulterated text of a philologist, but a text with a built-in intentionality to survive as a living work of art beyond the historical and geographical boundaries of its first appearances, 'in states unborn and accents yet unknown', as Strehler says, quoting a line spoken by Cassius in *Julius Caesar* (3.1.126). The text's intentionality to survive as a living work of art must triumph, even if survival entails being subjected to deforming misreadings, 'anche a costo di deformazioni' (Strehler 1989: 53).

If the term 'text' is understood to include scenarios as well as fully scripted plays, Strehler's observations can be applied verbatim to the commedia dell'arte, whose history and geography as well as its power of adaptation enabled it to move outwards and onwards from sixteenth-century Venice, Padua and Naples, reaching out to audiences in other countries and other centuries. In the twentieth century, a number of directors brought the commedia dell'arte up to date with respect to its power to communicate with modern audiences, and then took it abroad, where it could flourish in conjunction with local dramatic forms. The history of these efforts would deserve a large volume in itself. In this chapter we can only take into account the work of a few directors that illustrates clearly how the performance conventions of the commedia dell'arte were rediscovered, studied and enlisted to serve new theories of the stage.

Giorgio Strehler's *Arlecchino*

Theatre scholars have duly recognized the enormous contribution of Giorgio Strehler to world theatre, but it is no doubt his production of Goldoni's *Servitore di due padroni* that first brought him to the attention of the international public. Since 1947, when the Piccolo Teatro di Milano presented it as the closing play of its first season, Strehler's production has toured throughout the world and is still in the Piccolo's active repertoire, long after his death (1997). Throughout the years, the production has changed – in the parlance of the Piccolo, it has been given in several 'editions' – but the assumption that it is a single unchanging production is common. Strehler changed the name of Goldoni's Truffaldino to the more easily recognizable Arlecchino and modified the title of the play to read *Arlecchino servitore di due padroni,* usually abbreviated as 'Strehler's *Arlecchino*' or 'Strehler's *Harlequin*' in English. In 1995, when the production was almost forty years old, Strehler in an interview welcomed the opportunity to correct the misconception about his staging of Goldoni's play, pointing out that there had already been 'at least 6 different versions' with different actors (Strehler 1996: 273). Actually, depending on how difference in versions is gauged, the final count is higher. According to Gabrielle Houle, by 1997 there were ten productions, which had been performed 2,394 times in thirty-six countries (2017: 7). In this half-century of production history (1947–97), only two actors played Harlequin: Marcello Moretti and Ferruccio Soleri, who had been Moretti's apprentice and understudy.

Though some of the actors and some design features were different, all of these productions had one trait in common: in all of them, Strehler displayed more interest in the early conventions of commedia dell'arte than was warranted by Goldoni's text. At the same time, however, Strehler increasingly presented those conventions in the frame of modern epic theatre. The performance text that he brought to the public, especially in the later editions, has a double aesthetic orientation away from the mid-eighteenth century: it simultaneously looks backwards to the commedia dell'arte that preceded Goldoni's reform and forwards to the conventions of epic drama. Strehler read Goldoni's text through performance techniques of early commedia dell'arte and staged it on a set that showcased the actors sitting by the wings chatting or watching the play in the dispassionate style of epic drama until they heard their cues. The performance area itself was a raised trestle platform duplicating a primitive booth stage in a piazza with a painted curtain as background. The epic structuring principle was made especially clear in the edition which premiered at the Edinburgh International Festival of 1956 (Bosisio 2005: 12).

The commedia and epic aspects of the production were united by a visual narrative, depicting a troupe of itinerant actors in the act of performing Goldoni's play in a piazza. In essence, Strehler's *Harlequin* has an epic framing action on the side benches and a framed commedia dramatic action on the inner stage. The audience was placed 'before a double show', recalls Ferruccio Soleri (in Gorla 2005: 31). The epic framing, silent though it was, calls attention, in the guise of a poetics of staging, to Strehler's retrieval of commedia dell'arte from within a dominant form of modern theatre.

Chief among the staging techniques of Strehler's *Harlequin* are, first, the quick tempo at which stage action was to be carried out in scenes that required to-and-fro movement, a fact facilitated by the dimensions of the platform stage, which was much smaller than the stage itself and could hence be crossed very quickly, giving the impression of a whirlwind of activity; second, the physical *lazzi* that had to be performed, enhancing the effect of acrobatic buffoonery; and third, the Sartori masks with which the actors had to play, which emphasized the primitive nature and animalistic roots of the main stock characters. By means of such details, Strehler made a much greater contribution to our knowledge of commedia dell'arte and its appropriation by epic drama than he did to our understanding of Goldoni.

In the first half of the twentieth century, the dominant performance tradition of the commedia dell'arte was to play Harlequin without a mask, despite the wealth of historical iconography showing him with a mask. Almost as if prompted by Goldoni's *Teatro comico*, the acting profession of the twentieth century had moved decidedly away from masks in favour of social and psychological realism. Strehler did not agree with this trend, and, when he first cast Moretti as Harlequin, he asked him to perform the character wearing a mask. Upon witnessing Moretti's inability to act with a mask, and upon hearing his passionate arguments against its use on the modern stage – arguments recently examined with considerable rigour by Gabrielle Houle (2017) – Strehler allowed him to perform Harlequin with heavy make-up in the shape of a mask, advising him, however, to explore the advantages of masked performance. Moretti followed Strehler's advice and kept experimenting with his mask, slowly discovering its expressive potential and changing his perspective on what could be regarded as authentic commedia style acting. By observing Moretti come to terms with his mask, slowly mastering its use in the expression of feelings, attitudes and the like, Strehler was able to catalogue the expressive range of masks and hence come to understand their fundamental role in the performance conventions of the early commedia dell'arte and in his own productions. In the improvisation of dialogue, consisting of words and gestures, masks play a compositional role of some significance. Strehler and Moretti could not attain such knowledge by simply examining written sources, and so they used the rehearsal stage as a research laboratory. Strehler characterized the fruit of their research as a rediscovery and appropriation of commedia conventions by modern actors, because 'it was a matter of re-inventing' techniques that had been lost and re-establishing their vitality in the present (Strehler 1980: 3).

In reviewing Moretti's growing intimacy with his mask, Strehler made a few important observations about commedia dell'arte masks in general. Since they are really half-masks, they leave the mouth and the chin visible and mobile, a fact that gives the mouth a great capacity of gestural expression well beyond the words that it utters. When they do not wear a mask, actors may touch their noses, rub their eyes, cover their faces with both hands, performing the same kinds of gestures that they routinely make in real life. Such realistic gestures have no place in commedia style acting simply because masks are inconsistent with natural gestures. The mask is a powerful and unnatural instrument. It places the actor on the boundary between concrete reality and a mysterious region of the imagination whence re-emerge, with their unchanging faces, the demons and spirits of primeval rituals. Masks cannot be integrated with naturalistic gestures in performance. On stage, an actor cannot touch his mask as if touching his uncovered face because that would undermine the function of the mask. All gestures of touching can be no more than stylized, suggestive indications, performed with the fingers at some distance from the surface of the mask (Strehler 1979: 273).

In order to help Moretti come to terms with Harlequin's mask, Strehler began a close collaboration with the sculptor Amleto Sartori, who had rediscovered and taught himself the ancient art of making masks, as practised by the seventeenth century artisans who created leather masks for commedia dell'arte actors. On the basis of theatre iconography and Renaissance physiognomy, which represented human temperaments in terms of the facial resemblance between animals and people (Sartori and Lanata 1984: 31), Sartori had theorized that Harlequin's mask could be sculpted to suggest a cat, a fox or a bull, depending on the temperament by which the character's behaviour seemed to be governed. Moretti experimented with all these masks in order to find the one that could enable him to represent Harlequin in the most authentic way possible for him. In the end he decided on a feline mask with large eye holes, which did not impede his lateral vision and enabled him to develop a movement style appropriate to his vision of the character as an inventive and clever manipulator of the situation.

This quest for authentic commedia performance techniques proved to be highly significant, technically and aesthetically for the actor, and hermeneutically for directors, dramaturgs and scholars, who thereby were able to discover something about commedia dell'arte that they could not do without using the rehearsal room as a research laboratory. Moretti and Strehler had 'to uncover the techniques of the improvised commedia' by probing the semiotic range of its masks in the act of performance (Strehler 1980: 3). The research project was at once investigative and constructive: it was meant to help them understand the commedia dell'arte in the context of the material conditions of its performance in the seventeenth

century so that they could shape their own performance style
in the twentieth.

Giovanni Poli's neo-commedia

Throughout the twentieth century, a number of other directors,
including some of the protagonists of avante-garde dramaturgy,
turned to the commedia dell'arte, confident that there they
could find an authentic antecedent of the kind of theatre that
they were struggling to establish. Among the lesser figures, we
find Giovanni Poli, founder of the Teatro all'Avogaria in Venice
(1969) as a venue where he could experiment with dramatic
forms and performance techniques derived from the primary
historical sources of the commedia dell'arte but interpreted
from the perspective of avante-garde theories of the stage.
From the welter of material left by Poli – archival documents
and little-known published works, recently gathered and made
available by Giulia Filacanapa in a convenient anthology (Poli
2015) – we know that at the heart of Poli's mature research
project is the idea of a commedia dell'arte mask. It was chiefly
on the basis of what masks did for players in the past that
Poli developed his neo-commedia (Filacanapa's term) for
the present, except that now the actors had a full script and
their commedia masks could be leveraged against various
dramaturgies of realism.

Masks distinguish characters from real human beings and
liberate actors from the aesthetic presupposition that the
criterion of artistic success is naturalistic imitation. Masks
enabled the improvisatory players of historical commedia
dell'arte, and can now enable the players of neo-commedia,
to transform dramatic characters from copies of reality into
abstract social types that could be easily used as instruments
of ideological discourse. Consistently with this understanding
of masks, voice must also be liberated from the need to
reproduce the rhythm and cadence of real conversations. The

performers then should strive to express sentiments vocally without copying reality. Voice should distinguish them aurally from real people just as masks distinguish them visually. Similarly, gesture should not be anchored to the idea that all movement must be natural. On the contrary, gesture should be governed by the rhythm of the voice and strive to give physical expression to the sentiment conveyed by the words, themselves pronounced non-naturalistically under the alienating power of the mask (Poli 2015: 370).

For Poli these ideas were inherent in all the masked characters of unscripted commedia dell'arte, all of whom could be regarded as variants of the original *zanni,* as he made clear in his play *La commedia degli zanni*, a veritable 'manifesto-show' according to Filacanapa (2015: 383). The performance techniques of the actors impersonating them could be studied by examining historical sources, including iconography, but the task of neo-commedia was not to mimic the old commedia dell'arte on the avante-garde stage, but to put the knowledge thus obtained into the creation of a new theatre. The avante-garde director could use the conceptual base and performance techniques of early *zanni* to develop a new dramaturgy for and of the present and beyond. Such a dramaturgy presupposes an aesthetic vision of the stage that looks backwards and forwards at the same time. For directors like Poli, the objective was not to revive the early commedia dell'arte in its original form, transplanting the distant past into the present, but to learn from it what possibilities for the future lay at hand in the here and now of history.

Mazzone-Clementi's commedia pedagogy in the New World

The here and now of history was also central to Carlo Mazzone-Clementi's view of commedia dell'arte, although in his case 'here' means California, specifically the small town of Blue Lake, where he started the Dell'Arte School of Mime and Comedy (1972), from which later emerged the Dell'Arte Players company (Berson 1983: 62). Mazzone-Clementi designed the training programme of the company and taught commedia dell'arte performance techniques in a way that reflected both their historical roots and their suitability for a modern vision of the theatre. Mazzone-Clementi had brought with him knowledge of the early history of commedia dell'arte, familiarity with Marcel Marceau and Jacques Lecoq, with both of whom he had worked as a young performer in Italy, and an intimate knowledge of the commedia masks of Amleto Sartori. He brought together these three areas of expertise into the creation of a one-man show as a teaching tool, in which he played the roles of the principal masked characters of the commedia tradition. His objective was to teach the principles of performance mastered by the original players of the commedia dell'arte but reshaped in a way that made them available to modern American performers interested in creating an indigenous form of commedia dell'arte.

As a practitioner, he was not especially interested in the academic study of commedia dell'arte documents, an approach that he regarded as 'shallow and limiting' (Mazzone-Clementi 1974: 64), but in what those documents could reveal about the art of acting, though, of course, they had other things to say to researchers concerned with other aspects of theatre history. The commedia dell'arte, he observed, is like a drawer full of different things, from which researchers select what they find most appealing (59). Among the things that he pulled out, the first consisted of the rules of etiquette governing the relationship between the actors and their audience. His approach to the study of commedia dell'arte was to begin with the types of actors employed in a company. There were three kinds, which he called *caricati*, *macchiette* and *maschere*, each entrusted with the responsibility of commanding a certain portion of the audience's attention and of eliciting a certain degree of applause. The *caricati* were actors who played caricatured characters, such as the lovers, and in doing so were expected to provoke some laughter and elicit some applause; the *macchiette* (literally, little spots) were actors specializing in cameo roles, interesting and funny in themselves for their distinguishing features, who were expected to entertain the audience for brief periods of time; *maschere* were the actors who played the masked characters, fundamental to all commedia dell'arte plays and responsible for eliciting a grand response in each performance. These rules of company etiquette, according to Mazzone-Clementi, tacitly governed the internal professional dynamics of typical commedia dell'arte companies.

The second thing that Mazzone-Clementi pulled out of the commedia drawer was the performance pedagogy presupposed or implied by the way that the actors impersonated the masked characters. For him the foundation of this pedagogy was the idea of the human body, centred on the spine. All modern commedia training must begin with the spine and move outward to all other parts of the body. Writing under the influence of Jacques Lecoq and Marcel Marceau, Mazzone-Clementi emphasized movement to the point that he regarded a character's style of movement as his main identifying trait. In movement training, authentic commedia masks, such as those designed and made by Amleto Sartori, are necessary because, while they conceal facial gestures, they enable the actor to discover the expressive uniqueness of the character.

A third significant principle that can be learned from historical commedia dell'arte sources is the thought-provoking potential of its silly masked characters. According to Mazzone-Clementi, they are based on the idea that the village fool can be used as 'a point of departure for understanding mankind' (60). Commedia dell'arte humour, in other words, has a cognitive dimension, and performance, while entertaining with silliness, is also a serious means of reflection on human nature from the perspective of the folk culture that produced the masked characters. When it is brought into focus in the context of possible analogies with distant folk cultures, this principle can have far-reaching implications, both aesthetic and cognitive. Working with the analogy, suggested by Mazzone-Clementi, between commedia masked characters and the animal spirits of native American culture – an analogy no doubt inspired by Sartori masks sculpted to suggest animal behaviour (Houle 2017: 132) – the Dell'Arte Players sought out some of these implications in 1975 in a performance-generating research project that led Jael Weisman, Joan Holden and Steve Most to write for them *The Loon's Rage* (Berson 1983: 63; Schirle 2015: 394). This play, the first of the Dell'Arte Players, harmoniously combines native American ideas and commedia dell'arte conventions, thus showing how, creatively transplanted into the new world, commedia dell'arte could become a naturalized expression of contemporary American theatre culture.

Commedia tricks in the *giullarate* of Dario Fo

The line 'in states unborn and accents yet unknown', cited by Strehler from *Julius Caesar*, is a good point of access to the theatre of Dario Fo and its roots in the commedia dell'arte. In the long and complex trajectory of his career, which goes from clown to Nobel Prize winner, Dario Fo has always acknowledged his relationship to the commedia dell'arte, though not in the style of Strehler. He regarded Strehler's *Harlequin* as a great lesson in the art of directing commedia, but the commedia that interested him most was a more primitive version of the *zanni* than Strehler made use of in his interpretation of Goldoni's play. Ever since his early years as a professional player, Dario Fo, together with his wife, the very talented actress Franca Rame, practised a form of physical and political theatre that made use of many commedia dell'arte conventions (Fido 1995). It was only in his theoretical work *Manuale minimo dell'attore* (1987), translated as *The Tricks of the Trade* (1991), that he explicitly reviewed the conventions of commedia dell'arte performances relevant to his *Mistero buffo* (1969) or comical mystery play, in which he leveraged them into the creation of his most congenial dramatic form, the comic *giullarata*. Though it was published after *Mistero buffo*, *The Tricks of the Trade* synthesized fundamental principles of Fo's stage practice over many years, including the period before and after the appearance of his famous *giullarata*. Among the things that interested him most from the commedia dell'arte tradition were the centrality of gestures and the importance of dialects in the process of improvisation.

In *The Tricks of the Trade* Dario Fo laments the fact that in actor training programmes, as in the teaching of language to children, gestures were generally relegated to a 'secondary position' (35). He argues strongly for their centrality in theatrical communication and refers to the commedia dell'arte for supporting evidence. From the commedia dell'arte we learn that masks are essential to gesture pedagogy because they compel the students to discover how to communicate with their bodies rather than their faces and eyes. But whether in masked or unmasked performance, gestures are not only physical ways of conveying ideas but also a mechanism for directing and focusing the attention of the audience. In one-man shows, for example, it is essential to keep all gestures close to the body, extending them no more than 30 cm. Beyond this limit, the audience loses its focus on the performer and its interest in the action performed (45).

To achieve credibility in the representation of the kind of character that interested Fo, namely the early *zanni* of commedia dell'arte and the peasants of Ruzante as types of the downtrodden of all ages, particularly the present, the best language to turn to in Italy was the dialect spoken at home and not the Italian language, which, for the vast majority of Italians of Fo's generation, was not the mother tongue but a second language first acquired in primary school. The dialects were the mother tongues, and the more archaically pronounced the more effective they were on stage. Considered in the context of the literary Italian of the audience, dialects have a peculiar phonology, a cadence, a rhythm and a repertory of vocal gestures capable of making the sonic substance of speech aesthetically engaging and highly communicative. Dialects connote provenance from a culture perceived by the audience as low and unsophisticated, and marked by a total absence of that refinement of spirit that is assumed to come from formal education based on written sources. Dialect belongs to the culture of orality, which has its own sophistication. Its sounds and words articulate an experience of reality, social and otherwise, that is necessarily distinct from that of languages grounded in literacy, an experience that cannot be easily rendered in literate languages.

If one proceeds to remove the semantic component of words from a speech in dialect, the sonic material that remains, structured by the natural rhythm and cadence that the dialect exhibits when it is properly spoken, can give the impression of a meaningful and precise utterance without actually saying anything that could be translated *ad verbum* into a natural language. Meaning, however, can be articulated and conveyed by inserting into the utterance the odd easily understood word and onomatopoeic syllables. The resulting flow of sounds may include gibberish but carries meaning nonetheless. The idiom obtained by such a manipulation of sounds, linguistic and otherwise, is a *grammelot*, the term that Dario Fo borrows from seventeenth-century French commedia dell'arte, suggesting that he retrieved directly from it. The facts are a little more complicated than he lets on, as Erith Jaffe-Berg has shown. The very quest for the term may have been suggested to Dario Fo by *grummelotage,* the term by which Jacques Coupeau designated a training exercise using the words of an invented language while miming a real one (Jaffe-Berg 2009: 105). *Grammelot* is a naturally sounding invented idiom that expresses the speaker's intended meaning while comically theatricalizing the dialect, the culture and the inventiveness of the speaker. The same operation can be carried out with and in any spoken language that is foreign to the audience. A language can be mimicked by its own *grammelot*.

The linguistic base of the *giullarate* included in *Mistero buffo* is a mixture of dialects from the Po Valley in Northern

Italy, reminiscent at once of the vernacular of the storytellers that Dario Fo heard as a boy in rural Lombardy and of the phonology of the same dialects reconstructed from early Renaissance sources. Derived from *giullare*, the term for a street performer and storyteller in the popular culture of the late Middle Ages, a *giullarata* is the dramatic form of a one-man show in which the actor gives expression to the way the uneducated poor experience the culture that has come down to the audience through the intellectual lens of the elite. *Mistero buffo* is a collection of texts for such performances, in which the actor is required to play, without set and costume, the role of a *giullare* in the act of telling a story and the roles of the dialoguing characters in the story itself, using gestures, Italian, dialect and *grammelot*. In a *giullarata* there are two different modes of acting: a primary one in which the storyteller is represented by the actor in Italian, and a secondary one in which the characters are represented by the storyteller in dialect and *grammelot*. The secondary mode is clearly more complex, calling as it does for the actor to perform both the narrator and the character at the same time, with a single issue of his voice and precise gestures, both physical and vocal.

In *Mistero buffo*, the ratio between the narrative and the dialogic components of a *giullarata* varies considerably from one story to the other. In *The Resurrection of Lazarus* the narrative component in indirect speech is absent. There is only the direct speech of a multitude of speakers, which give it a polyphonic character (Piccolo 1988: 137). The narrator's voice can be heard only as it pronounces words spoken by the sixteen different characters involved in the story, much of which flows at a very fast tempo. Since the *giullare* must play all the characters without interrupting the action with narrative comments, Dario Fo regarded *The Resurrection of Lazarus* as a very difficult text, going as far as to say in his introduction that it requires the skill of a virtuoso (Fo 1977: 96). The actor should not attempt to change the timbre of his voice or move around the stage but should limit himself to body language and voice modulation, to signal the entrance of a new speaking character and to convey, without describing it as a narrator, the idea of a crowd of spectators building up in the cemetery around the grave of Lazarus, where they are about to witness Jesus performing a great miracle. The actor must hence perform the individual characters, the space around them and the choral crescendo of excitement and impatience, all the while observing the audience and calibrating his vocal and gestural language by their response.

This highly sophisticated mode of performance, Fo observes, comes to the *giullarata* from the commedia dell'arte. *The Resurrection of Lazarus* compels the actor to perform 'a soggetto', that is, by improvising on a 'canovaccio' or scenario. As in conventional commedia dell'arte, the performance text will vary from one evening to the next because no two improvisations can be exactly alike. The crucial factor, Fo points out, is the actor's skill in letting the flow of his improvisation be guided by the rhythm and duration of the audience's response with laughter or silence (Fo 1977: 96). But as was the practice in commedia dell'arte improvisations, the *giullarata* performer must remain within the narrative confines of the story, which are invisible constraints on his improvisation. In the analysis of *The Resurrection of Lazarus* that he included in *The Tricks of the Trade*, Dario Fo explains that gestures can communicate by allusion rather than by imitation: bending a little towards the audience as if pushed from behind alludes to the presence of a growing crowd pressing to get closer to the grave and places the grave in front of the speaker. Asking a question and answering it without pause by making a slight movement of the face alludes to the presence of another character. In a *giullarata* such actions, Fo explains, are analogous to cross-cuttings in cinema, which give the impression of two actions taking place at the same time (Fo 1991: 94).

By a simple combination of gesture and voice, a character can thus evoke the image of another character entering the performance, either in the same location or in another area of the textual space of the action. The *giullare* orientates the gaze of the audience, widens its field of vision, and directs its focus on a detail, as if he were manipulating by remote control a camera hidden in their heads (Fo 1991: 44). What is more, if the *giullare* turns to the audience and raises his voice while impersonating a character speaking to another, he can project the listening character into the audience and expand the textual space of the action until it coincides with the auditorium. By speaking to a single character among the spectators, he thereby addresses them all, as if they had a collective role to play in the dramatic action. This is how the *giullare* draws them onto the stage, casting them in the role of bystanders, observing the grand miracle, witnessing the way the people experience it, and hearing how the speak about it, in accents yet unknown.

REFERENCES

Alighieri, Dante (1966). *La Commedia*, a cura di Giorgio Petrocchi.
Milano: Mondadori.

Ambros, Veronika (2012). 'Puppets, Statues, Men, Objects and the
Prague School', *Theatralia* 15.2: 74–88.

Andrews, Richard (1993). *Scripts and Scenarios: The Performance of
Comedy in Renaissance Italy*. Cambridge: Cambridge University
Press.

Andrews, Richard (2008). *The Commedia dell'Arte of Flaminio
Scala: A Translation and Analysis of 30 Scenarios*. Lanham, MD,
Toronto, Plymouth, UK: Scarecrow Press.

Aristotle (1954). *Poetics*, trans. Ingram Bywater, in *Rhetoric and
Poetics of Aristotle*, ed. Friedrich Solmsen. New York, NY:
Random House Modern Library.

Barber, Benjamin (2007). *Consumed: How Markets Corrupt
Children, Infantalize Adults and Swallow Citizens Whole*. New
York, NY: Norton.

Barbieri, Niccolò (1634). *La Supplica*. Venezia: Marco Ginammi.

Baricci, Erica (2010). 'La scena "all'ebraica" nel teatro del
rinascimento', *Annali della Facoltà di Lettere e Filosofia
dell'Università degli Studi di Milano* 63.1: 135–63.

Bartoli, Adolfo (1979). *Scenari inediti della commedia dell'arte*.
Bologna: Forni [1st edn, 1880].

Bartolomei, Girolamo (1658). *Didascalia cioè dottrina comica*.
Firenze: Stamperia Nuova.

Battistella, Antonio (1979). 'Diario di un attore', in Carlo Goldoni,
Arlecchino servitore di due padroni, ed. Luigi Lunari et al.,
214–68. Milano: Rizzoli.

Beolco, Angelo (1994). *L'Anconitana: The Woman from Ancona*,
trans. Nancy Dersofi. Berkeley and Los Angeles, CA: University
of California Press.

Berson, Misha (1983). 'The Dell'Arte Players of Blue Lake,
California', *The Drama Review* 27.2: 61–72.

Biancolelli, Domenico (1978). *Le festin de pierre*, in Marcello
   Spaziani, *Don Giovanni dagli scenari dell'arte alla foire*, 135–50.
   Roma: Edizioni di Storia e Letteratura.

[Bignon, Édouard-Alexandre (1806)]. *L'orang-outang ovvero l'uomo
   del bosco incivilito.* [n.p.].

Bosisio, Paolo (2005). 'A Clapping of Hands as Large as the World',
   in *Arlecchino servitore di due padroni*, United States Tour, 8–15.
   Milan: Piccolo Teatro di Milano and Teatro d'Europa.

Bragaglia, Anton Giulio (1959). *Giangurgolo, ovvero il Calabrese in
   commedia*. Cosenza: Ente Provinciale del Turismo.

Buckley, Matthew (2009). 'The Body and Meaning in Early
   Commedia dell'Arte', *Theatre Survey* 50.2: 251–315.

Busoni, Ferruccio (1950). *Arlecchino, oder Die Fenster*. Wiesbaden:
   Breitkopf & Härtel.

Busoni, Ferruccio (1962). *Sketch of a New Esthetic of Music*, in
   Three Classics in the Aesthetic of Music: Debussy, Ives, Busoni.
   New York, NY: Dover.

Cammarano, Filippo (1824). *Le cento disgrazie di Pulcinella
   perseguitato da donne nutrice*. Napoli: D'Ambra.

Capozza, Nicoletta (2006). *Tutti i lazzi della commedia dell'arte*.
   Roma: Audino Editore.

Cappelletti, Salvatore (1986). *Luigi Riccoboni e la riforma del
   teatro*. Ravenna: Longo.

Casamarciano Scenarios (2001). Francesco Cotticelli, Anne
   Goodrich Heck and Thomas F. Heck (eds), *The Commedia
   dell'arte in Naples: A Bilingual Edition of the 176 Casamarciano
   Scenarios*. Lanham, MD, and London: The Scarecrow Press.

Castagno, Paul (1994). '*Mente teatrale*: Andrea Calmo and the
   Victory of the Performance Text in Cinquecento *commedia*',
   Journal of Dramatic Theory and Criticism Spring: 37–57.

Cecchini, Pier Maria (1628). *Frutti delle moderne commedie et avisi
   a chi le recita*. Padova: Guaresco Guareschi.

Cole, Toby and Helen Krich Chinoy, eds (1970). *Actors on Acting*.
   New York, NY: Crown.

Croce, Benedetto (1891). *I teatri di Napoli, secolo XV–XVIII*.
   Napoli: Presso Luigi Pierro.

Crohn Schmitt, Natalie (2014). *Befriending the Commedia dell'Arte
   of Flaminio Scala*. Toronto: University of Toronto Press.

Crohn Schmitt, Natalie (2020). *Performing Commedia dell'Arte*.
   London and New York, NY: Routledge.

Cruciani, Gianfranco (2004). *Vergilio Verrucci da Norcia: Commediografo del Seicento*. Arrone (Terni): Thyrrus.

Cuppone, Roberto (2001). '*In questo*: Il teatro e gli scenari della commedia dell'arte', *Transformação* 24: 121–41.

D'Antonio, Giovanne detto il Partenopeo (1788). *Scola cavajola*, in *Opere*, 191–204. Napoli: Presso Giuseppe-Maria Porcelle.

Da Ponte, Lorenzo (1990). *Don Giovanni*, in *Tre libretti per Mozart*. Milano: Rizzoli.

DeJean, Joan (1991). *Tender Geographies: Women and the Origin of the Novel in France*. New York, NY: Columbia University Press.

Della Porta, Giambattista (1615). *La trappolaria*. Ferrara: Baldini Stampatore Camerale.

Everaert-Desmedt, Nicole. (1989). *Sémiotique du récit*. Brussels: De Boeck-Wesmael.

Einstein, Alfred (1938). 'Concerning Some Recitatives in *Don Giovanni*', *Music and Letters* 19.4: 417–25.

Eldredge, Sears A. (1996). *Mask Improvisation for Actor-Training & Performance*. Evanston, IL: Northwestern University Press.

Ferrone, Siro (1985). *Commedie dell'Arte*. Milano: Mursia.

Ferrone, Siro (2014). *La Commedia dell'Arte: Attrici e attori italiani in Europa (XVI–XVIII secolo)*. Torino: Einaudi.

Fido, Franco (1973). 'An Introduction to the Theater of Angelo Beolco', *Renaissance Drama*, new series, 6: 203–18.

Fido, Franco (1995). 'Dario Fo e la Commedia dell'Arte', *Italica* 72.3: 298–306.

Filacanapa, Giulia (2015). 'Giovanni Poli: The Missing Link', in *The Routledge Companion to Commedia dell'Arte*, ed. Judith Chaffe and Olly Crick, 378–85. London and New York, NY: Routledge.

Fischer-Lichte, Erika (1992). *The Semiotics of Theater*. Bloomington, IN: Indiana University Press.

Fitzpatrick, Tim (1989). 'Flaminio Scala's Prototypal Scenarios: Segmenting the Text/Performance', in Pietropaolo (1989), 177–98.

Fo, Dario (1977). *Le Commedie: Mistero buffo, Ci ragiono e ci canto*. Torino: Einaudi.

Fo, Dario (1991). *The Tricks of the Trade*, trans. Joe Farrell, ed. Stuart Hood. New York, NY: Routledge.

Fowler, Jim (2010). 'Hester Santlow: Harlequin Lady', in *The World of Baroque Theatre: A Compilation of Essays from the Cesky*

Krumlov Conferences 2007–2009, 2009, 47–52. Cesky Krumlov, Baroque Theatre Foundation.

Gentilcore, David (2006). *Medical Charlatanism in Early Modern Italy.* Oxford: Oxford University Press.

Gherardi, Évariste (1741). *Le théâtre italien de Gherardi,* vol. 1, Paris: Briasson.

Gherardi, Évariste (1970). 'On the Art of Italian Comedians', in Toby Cole and Helen Krich Chinoy, eds, *Actors on Acting,* 57–9. New York, NY: Crown.

Goldoni, Carlo (1761). *Delle commedie di Carlo Goldoni avvocato Veneto,* vol. 12. Venezia: Giambattista Pasquali.

Goldoni, Carlo (1877). *Memoirs,* trans. J. Black, ed. W. D. Howells. Boston, MA: James R. Osgood and Company.

Goldoni, Carlo (1967). *Il servitore di due padroni,* a cura di Guido Davico Bonino. Torino: Einaudi.

Goldoni, Carlo (1969). *The Comic Theatre,* trans. John W. Miller. Lincoln, NE: University of Nebraska press.

Goldoni, Carlo (1983). *Il teatro comico* e *memorie italiane,* a cura di Guido Davico Bonino. Milano: Mondadori.

Goldoni, Carlo (1993). *Memorie, con un appendice di scritti goldoniani,* a cura di Guido Davico Bonino. Torino: Einaudi.

Goldoni, Carlo (1996). *Arlecchino servitore di due padroni,* a cura di Carlo Pedretti. Milano: Rizzoli.

Gordon, Mel (1983). *Lazzi: The Comic Routines of the Commedia dell'Arte.* New York, NY: Performing Arts Journal.

Gori, Domenico (1604). *Trattato contro alle commedie lascive,* in Ferdinando Taviani (1969), *La Commedia dell'Arte e la società barocca: La fascinazione del teatro,* 136–43. Roma: Bulzoni.

Gorla, Matteo (2005). 'Ferruccio Soleri Recounts *Harlequin*', in *Arlecchino servitore di due padroni,* United States Tour, 29–31. Milan: Piccolo Teatro di Milano and Teatro d'Europa.

Gozzi, Carlo (1890). 'A Reflective Analysis of the Fable Entitled *The Love of the Three Oranges*', in *The Memoirs of Count Carlo Gozzi,* trans. John Addington Symonds, 112–46. London: Scribner and Welford.

Gozzi, Carlo (1962). *Opere,* ed. Giuseppe Petronio. Milano: Rizzoli.

Gozzi, Carlo (2021). *Reflective Analysis of the Fairy Tale 'The Love of Three Oranges*', trans., introduced and annotated by Maria De Simone, in *Three Loves for Three Oranges: Gozzi, Meyerhold, Prokofiev,* ed. Dassia N. Posner, Kevin Bartig and Maria De Simone, 92–107. Bloomington, IN: Indiana University Press.

Gundel, Jeannette K. and Thorstein Fretheim (2009). 'Information Structure', in *Grammar, Meaning and Pragmatics*, ed. Frank Brisard, Jan-Ola Östman and Jef Verschueren, 146–60. Amsterdam and Philadelphia, PA: John Benjamins Publishing Company.

Heck, T. F. (1988). *Commedia dell'Arte: A Guide to the Primary and Secondary Literature*. New York, NY, and London: Garland Publishing.

Henke, Robert (2002). *Performance and Literature in the Commedia dell'Arte*. Cambridge: Cambridge University Press.

Henke, Robert (2016). 'Meeting at the Sign of the Queen: The Commedia dell'Arte, Cheap Print, and Piazza Performance', *Italian Studies* 71.2: 171–83.

Herrick, Marvin J.(1964). *Comic Theory in the Sixteenth Century*. Urbana, IL: University of Illinois Press.

Hofmannsthal, Hugo von (2017). *Ariadne auf Naxos*, neuausgabe mit einer Biographie des Autors Herausgegeben von Karl-Maria Guth. Der Text dieser Ausgabe folgt *Gesammelte Werke in zehn Einzenbänden,* Band 1, *Gedichte, Dramen,* Herausgegeben von Bernd Schoeller in Beratung mit Rudolf Hirsch (Frankfurt 1979). Berlin: Contumax.

Hogarth, William (1753). *The Analysis of Beauty*. London: John Reeves.

Horace (1989). *Epistles*, Book II and *Epistle to the Pisones, Ars Poetica*, ed. Nial Rudd. Cambridge: Cambridge University Press.

Houle, Gabrielle (2017). 'Resisting Arlecchino's Mask: The Case of Marcello Moretti', *Theatre History Studies*, 36: 7–28.

Jaffe-Berg, Erith (2009). *The Multilingual Art of Commedia dell'Arte*. Ottawa: Legas.

Jaffe-Berg, Erith (2015). *Commedia dell'Arte and the Mediterranean: Charting Journeys and Mapping 'Others'*. Farnham, Surrey and Burlington, VT: Routledge.

Jones, Peter (2019). *Laughter and Power in the Twelfth Century*. Oxford: Oxford University Press.

Jordan, Peter (2014). *The Venetian Origins of the Commedia dell'Arte*. London and New York, NY: Routledge.

Katritzky, M. A. (2006). *The Art of Commedia: A Study in the Commedia dell'Arte 1560–1620 with Special Reference to the Visual Records*. Amsterdam and New York, NY: Editions Rodopi.

Kerr, Rosalind (2015). *The Rise of the Diva in the Sixteenth-Century Commedia dell'Arte Stage*. Toronto: University of Toronto Press.

Lambranzi, Gregorio (1716). *Nuova e curiosa scuola de' balli theatrali – neue und curieuse teatralische Tantzschule*. Nuremberg: n.p.

Lambranzi, Gregorio (1966). *New and Curious School of Theatrical Dancing*, ed. Cyril Beaumont. New York, NY: Dance Horizons.

Mackintosh, Iain (1993). *Architecture, Actor and Audience*. London and New York, NY: Routledge.

Mamczarz, Irene (1973). 'Introduzione', in Luigi Riccoboni, *Discorso della commedia all'improvviso e scenari inediti*, ed. Irene Mamczarz, xi–xlix. Milano: Il Polifilo.

Mancinelli, Gregorio (1807). *Le novantanove disgrazie di Pulcinella*, 2nd edn. Roma: Gio. Battista Cannetti.

Marulli, Giacomo (1877). *Guida pratica del dialetto napoletano*. Napoli: Stabilimento Grafido Partenopeo.

Mazzone-Clementi, Carlo (1974). 'Commedia and the Actor', *The Drama Review* 18.1: 59–64.

Megale, Teresa (2020). *Tra mare e terra: La commedia dell'arte nella Napoli spagnola (1575–1656)*. Roma: Bulzoni.

Miller Lewis, Elizabeth (1999). 'Hester Santlow's Harlequine: Dance, Dress, Status and Gender on the London Stage, 1706–1734', in *The Clothes that Wear Us: Essays on Dressing and Transgressing in Eighteenth-Century Culture*, ed. Jessica Munns and Penny Richards, 80–101. Newark, DE: University of Delaware Press.

Molinari, Cesare (1985). *La commedia dell'arte*. Milano: Mondadori.

Molinari, Cesare (1997). 'Attori-autori della Commedia dell'Arte', *Quaderns d'Italià* 2: 21–37.

Molinari, Cesare and Valeria Ottolenghi (1985). *Leggere il teatro*. Firenze: Vallecchi.

Moro, Anna (1993). 'A Semiotic Interpretation of the *Lazzi* of the *Commedia dell'Arte*', *Theatre Symposium* 1: 66–76.

M.R.P., Teologo degli Andreini (1604). *Trattato sopra l'arte comica cavato dall'opere di S. Tommaso e d'altri Santi*. Firenze: Volemar Timan Germano.

Nicoll, Allardyce (1976). *The World of Harlequin: A Critical Study of the Commedia dell'Arte*. Cambridge: Cambridge University Press.

Oreglia, Giacomo (1968). *The Commedia dell'Arte*, trans. Lovett F. Edwards, with an introduction by Evert Spronchorn. New York, NY: Hill and Wang.

Ottonelli, Giovanni Domenico (1648). *Della Christiana Moderatione del Theatro*, Libro Primo dettto: *La qualità delle commedie*. Firenze: Stamperia Antonio Bonardi.

Ottonelli, Giovanni Domenico (1649). *Della Christiana Moderatione del Theatro*, Libro Secondo detto: *La solutione de' nodi*. Firenze: Stamperia Antonio Bonardi.

Ottonelli, Giovanni Domenico (1652). *Della Christiana Moderatione del Theatro*, Libro detto: *L'instanza*. Firenze: Stamperia Gio. Antonio Bonardi.

Pareyson, Luigi (2009).*Problemi dell'estetica*, vol. 1, *Teoria*, ed. Marco Ravera. Milano: Mursia.

Paulson, William R. (1987). *Enlightenment, Romanticism and the Blind in France*. Princeton, NJ: Princeton University Press.

Perrucci, Andrea (2008 [1699]). *A Treatise on Acting from Memory and by Improvisation (1699) – Dell'arte rappresentativa premeditata ed all'improvviso*, bilingual edn, trans. and ed. Francesco Cotticelli, Anne Goodrich Heck and Thomas F. Heck. Lanham, MD, Toronto and Plymouth, UK: The Scarecrow Press.

Piccolo, Pina (1988). 'Dario Fo's *giullarate*: Dialogic Parables in the Service of the Oppressed', *Italica* 65.2: 131–43.

Pietropaolo, Domenico, ed. (1989). *The Science of Buffoonery: Theory and History of the Commedia dell'Arte*. Ottawa: Dovehouse Editions.

Pietropaolo, Domenico (2006). 'Authorship, Directing and the Dramaturgy of Translation in the Commedia dell'Arte Tradition', in *Directing and Authorship in Western Drama*, ed. Anna Migliarisi, 91–100. Ottawa: Legas.

Pietropaolo, Domenico (2016). *Semiotics and Pragmatics of Stage Improvisation*. London: Bloomsbury.

Pietropaolo, Domenico (2022). 'Stage Improvisation in the Commedia dell'Arte', in *The Routledge Handbook of Philosophy and Improvisation in The Arts*, ed. Alessandro Bertinetto and Marcello Ruta, 502–14. New York, NY, and Abingdon, Oxford: Routledge.

Pirrotta, Nino (1955). 'Commedia dell'Arte and Opera', *The Musical Quarterly* 41.3: 305–24.

Poli, Giovanni (2015). *Écrits sur le théâtre*, in Giulia Filacanapa, 'À la recherche d'un théâtre perdu: Giovanni Poli (1917–1979) et la néo-commedia dell'arte en Italie, entre tradition et expérimentation', Thèse de doctorat, Universitè Paris 8 and Università di Firenze, vol. 2, 'Annexes', 101–86.

Propp, Vladimir (2009). *On the Comic and Laughter*, ed. and trans. Jean-Patrick Debbèche and Paul Perron. Toronto: University of Toronto Press.

Rabin, Dana (2005). 'Drunkenness and Responsibility for Crime in the Eighteenth-Century', *Journal of British Studies* 44.3: 457–77.

Radulescu, Domnica (2012). *Women's Comedic Art as Social Revolution*. Jefferson, NC: McFarland & Co.

Rancière, Jacques (2006). *The Politics of Aesthetics*, ed. and trans. Gabriel Rockhill. London: Continuum.

Riccoboni, Louis (1728–31). *Histoire du théâtre italienne*. Paris: Chaubert.

Riccoboni, Louis (1736). *Reflexions sur la comedie et le genie de Moliere*. Paris: Veuve Pissot.

Riccoboni, Louis (1738). *Reflexions historiques et critiques sur les differens theatres de l'Europe*. Paris: Jacques Guerrin.

Riccoboni, Luigi (1973). *Discorso della commedia all'improvviso e scenari inediti*, ed. Irene Mamczarz. Milano: Il Polifilo.

Righelli, Francesco (1613). *Il Pantalone impazzito*. Viterbo: Appresso Girolamo Discepolo.

Riverso, Nicla (2016). 'Fighting Eve: Women on the Stage in Early Modern Italy', *Quaderni d'italianistica* 37.2: 23–47.

Roulston, Chris (2010). *Narrating Marriage in Eighteenth-Century England and France*. Farnham, Surrey: Ashgate.

Rudlin, John (1986). *Jacques Copeau*. Cambridge: Cambridge University Press.

Sacchi, Gennaro (1699). *La commedia smascherata*. Versavia: Collegio delle Scuole Pie.

Sartori, Donato and Bruno Lanata (1984). *Maschera e maschere*. Milano: Usher.

Scala, Flaminio (1976). *Il teatro della favole rappresentative*, a cura di Ferruccio Marotti. Milano: Edizioni Il Polifilo. 2 vols.

Schirle, Joan (2015). 'Arlecchino Appleseed: Or How Carlo Mazzone-Clementi Brought Commedia to the New World', in *The Routledge Companion to Commedia dell'Arte*, ed. Judith

Chaffe and Olly Crick, 386–98. London and New York, NY: Routledge.

Shakespeare, William (2011). *Julius Caesar*, ed. Barbara A. Mowat and Paul Werstine. London: Simon & Schuster, Folger Shakespeare Library.

Steele, Richard (1791). *The Theatre*, vol. 1, ed. John Nichols. London: Nichols.

Stoehr, Taylor (1969). 'Realism and Verisimilitude', *Texas Studies in Literature and Language* 11.3: 1269–88.

Strehler, Giorgio (1979). 'In margine al diario: Ricordo di Marcello Moretti', in Carlo Goldoni, *Arlecchino servitore di due padroni*, ed. Luigi Lunari et al., 269–78. Milano: Rizzoli.

Strehler, Giorgio (1980). 'Introduction: Artisan Poetry', in *The Commedia dell'Arte and the Masks of Amleto and Donato Sartori*, ed. Andrea Rauch. Florence: Usher.

Strehler, Giorgio (1989). *Incontro*. Toronto: Istituto Italiano di Cultura.

Strehler, Giorgio (1996). 'In Response to Questions put to Him by the Editors and Eli Malke, 4 October 1995', trans. Peter Snowdon, in *In Contact with the Gods? Directors Talk Theatre*, ed. Maria M. Delgado and Paul Heritage, 264–76. Manchester and New York, NY: Manchester University Press.

Taviani, Ferdinando (1969). *La Commedia dell'Arte e la società barocca: La fascinazione del teatro*. Roma: Bulzoni.

Taviani, Ferdinando (1982). 'Il segreto delle compagnie italiane note poi come Commedia dell'Arte', in Ferdinando Taviani and Mirella Schino, *Il segreto della Commedia dell'Arte*, 295–448. Firenze: Usher.

Taviani, Ferdinando and Mirella Schino (1982). *Il segreto della Commedia dell'Arte*. Firenze: Usher.

Tessari, Roberto (1981–4). *Commedia dell'Arte: La maschera e l'ombra*. Milano: Mursia.

Tessari, Roberto (2017). 'Commedia dell'arte e ciarlataneria: inter-relazioni e interferenze', *Rebento* 7: 297–326.

Toepfer, Karl (2019). *Pantomime: The History and Metamorphosis of a Theatrical Ideology*. San Francisco, CA: Vosuri Media.

Trott, David (2000). *Théâtre du XVIIIᵉ siècle*. Montpellier: Éditions Espaces.

Tylus, Jane (1997). 'Women at the Windows: *Commedia dell'arte* and Theatrical Practice in Early Modern Italy', *Theatre Journal* 49.3: 323–42.

Vazzoler Franco (2018). 'Introduzione: Per meritar la vostra cortesia', in Carlo Gozzi, *Versi per gli attori*, ed. Giulietta Bazoli and Franco Vazzoler, 9–30. Venice: Marsilio.

Waygand, Zina (2009). *The Blind in French Society from the Middle Ages to the Century of Louis Braille*, trans. Emily Jane Cohen. Stanford, CA: Stanford University Press.

Weaver, John (1712). *An Essay Towards an History of Dancing*. London: Jacob Tonson.

Weaver, John (1728). *The History of Mimes and Pantomimes*. London: Roberts and Dod.

Wilbourne, Emily (2016). *Seventeeth-Century Opera and the Sound of Commedia dell'Arte*. Chicago, IL: Chicago University Press.

INDEX

Italic page numbers indicate figures on those pages.